BETWEEN WIND *and* WATER

GERALD WARNER BRACE

BETWEEN WIND *and* WATER

With illustrations by the author

DOWN EAST MAGAZINE
Camden/Maine

*To my cruising companions of long ago
particularly to the memory of my brother Charlie
and to John Donaldson and Lincoln Fairley*

But onely here and there wee touched or have seene a little
the edges of those large dominions, which doe stretch themselves
into the Maine, God doth know how many thousand miles.

Captain John Smith

CONTENTS

PREFACE

THE TITLE OF THIS BOOK once carried warlike connotations. If a ship was struck and holed by enemy cannon shot at the exact point of her water line, she filled and sank. But my representations are wholly peaceful. The two pervading realities of the coast of Maine are wind and water, and between them people and boats live and flourish. Some shots were once fired in anger here, but for most of its history it has been a place of good will.

The memories and pictures may recall some of the ways that were pleasant and sustaining. The mood is somewhat valedictory because though the place itself remains visibly there, the sea and the rocks and the forest, the ways and habits are disappearing and in the future will vanish entirely. I write in the consciousness of such physical and human changes to come as history has never before dreamed of.

We have had almost too much reminiscence of the old bucolic days, but it is an indulgence forgivable in times of change. Sentiment, however, is always suspect. The mood of elegy and nostalgia is easy to adopt, and often expresses merely a personal soft-headedness that the world rightly rejects. Our modern temper in general is inclined to be cynical, and assumes that human nature is as bad at one time as another. And of course it sees the primitive country life of other times as quite irrelevant to the realities of the present.

But with all our contemporary tough-mindedness the question is still to be answered: what does man live for? Control of nature, mastery of the cosmos, which is what our world is mainly up to, fails to satisfy the longings of the human heart. It may be that we must in the end redesign and remake the heart.

Though I have tried to avoid the soft ground of sentimentality, and to be fair and truthful in sketching the windy and watery life of the coast, it is necessary to make certain confessions. I am not only a summer visitor in Maine, but I date from that old world of long and wholly carefree vacations from June to September when life had nothing better to offer than perfect idle freedom. It is a life now looked upon with disdain—and also I suspect with some envy. The world yearns for "freedom" and demonstrates in its cause without quite knowing what it really means, but the old ways offered a modest variety of freedoms that were very pleasant. The summer folk of my memory were quite happy with peace and beauty, and an almost Spartan simplicity. They lived plainly, relished the country pleasures, and learned the ways of boats and tides. They rowed and fished and sometimes sailed. They made friends, were called by their first names, and developed a lifelong devotion to their community. Their children and grandchildren continue in the same memory and hope, but the golden age of summer innocence has gone.

It is to be confessed too that our habit was puritanical. The flagrant indulgences, if any, were to be kept to a minimum and carried on in secret. In this ethic everyone, native and nonnative alike, agreed. Sin might flaunt itself at the big resorts, but we knew nothing about that: let them indulge in gold bathtubs and yachts as big as liners—they didn't count as people; they had no relevance to the essential business of living. In our simplicity we felt that restraint and self-control were the way to happiness. The fewer demands, we thought, the greater freedom. We had no intimation of the Freudian revelation that the virtue of the puritans was a more sinister evil than the sins of the unregenerate. The fact that we were on the whole happy in our self-imposed suppressions, and even free in a naïve sort of way, is simply one of the persistent delusions of the pre-Freudian world.

There is no doubt that time has shortened and hastened in recent years. The facts of speed are obvious, but mind and conscience have changed too. Everything must be done. Schools must keep all year. Scientists must be trained. The moon must be reached. In business and the professions the competition is relentless. Scholars must publish. And above all is a hovering sense of doom: if all this desperate and frantic work is not done, if we fail to reach the moon or discover the secret of life, then we perish as a nation and a culture. Every aspect of our world is in a state of crisis and unless something be done about it at once chaos will come again.

I see no real possibility of a more relaxed world.

Thoreau's notion of a man sauntering forth to his work in a wide halo of ease and leisure is hardly viable in the conditions of our day. Wordsworth accused his fellow countrymen of wasting their time getting and spending, and recommended a quest for the old gods of the sea instead—but that was long ago in another century. Things are a good deal worse now.

Whether they are worse forever is more than I know. Human ingenuity can do miracles. We plan for a future free of drudgery, free of all harshness, secure in comfort, insulated against and protected from natural forces, and it may be that eventually some higher level of philosophical and spiritual serenity will be attained. Who knows? It is fashionable to be gloomy, to think the worst of man's chances—but it always has been. Man seems to endure, at least—perhaps, as Frost put it, his hold on the planet is increasing by say a fraction of one per cent. But whatever future he may shape for himself, or rebuild out of the atomic essences, it will be a world never dreamed of by Wordsworth or Thoreau or the folk of old Maine.

As for the sketches themselves, the pictures and the writing both, they are personal and reminiscent rather than informative. More books already exist about Maine (and about everything else on earth) than anyone can read. All the facts of past and present are in print. But writers and painters always hope for something beyond the facts, some intimation of the spirit or inward significance of things. Great writers and painters are pure magicians; they make you believe in miracles. But everyone who writes or draws hopes for some sort of miracle too. Out of these commonplace facts, by some lucky chance, may come a few gleams and glimpses of the beautiful vanishing world of the downeast coast.

Deer Isle, Maine
July 21, 1965

BETWEEN WIND *and* WATER

ONE

THE COAST

And more than 200 Iles overgrowne with
good timber, of divers sorts of wood, which doe
make so many harbours as requireth a longer time
then I had, to be well discovered.

Captain John Smith

THE ROCKY LAND between Cape Elizabeth and East
Quoddy Head was once a country apart from other
countries. It was a watery and islanded little nation
a day-and-night voyage from anywhere else. East and
south of it the frontiers were the cold sea and the fog;
west and north, forest and bad roads. All passages were
sea passages. The chief port in and out of the region was
the city of Boston, a couple of hundred miles away to the
southwest ("up to the westward," they said). The inland
territory of farms and forests untouched by salt water
was in some ways quite different—in origin and speech
and habit.

The coastal country has been celebrated in history and
legend for its seamen and builders, but what set it apart
and gave it its special quality was its natural architecture.
From Cape Ann as you go north and east along the coast
you find long leagues of low sandy shore and few islands
and harbors. Portsmouth and York offer river mouths,

with the in-and-out rush of tides. Cape Porpoise gives an anchorage behind a cluster of islets. The other harbors of western Maine are almost useless for sea-going vessels. But east of Cape Elizabeth a whole new geography opens out, with uncounted islands, bays, channels, big harbors, and little gunk holes. Whittier understated it when he struck off the resonant line, "Oh hundred-harbored Maine." There are thousands, if you count every nook and pocket where a boat can lie in safety; there are wondrous little secret holes, some in the very roll and surge of breakers yet secure in their quietness, some far from the open sea, up among the estuaries where tide rises and falls twice a day and no other motion disturbs the silences. A man could found a little kingdom for himself, apart from the known world, with all he needed for shelter and security, with fish and clams all about, and clean granite shores and good timber. He could keep a sloop-boat or schooner for himself—he could carry his bushels of clams to market, or load up his vessel with salt mackerel and set sail for Boston. He could become proprietor and hereditary lord of an island, and maintain whatever customs and laws he saw fit. Or he could live among neighbors in a larger community with a harbor busy with big and little vessels.

A coast for pirates and outlaws, you'd think. You can explore it for most of a lifetime and still find secret places —like the deep estuaries of Little Kennebec Bay, say, or along the lonely shores of Great Wass Island, or Pigeon Hill Bay, or the Bagaduce, or among the clustered islands outside the Musselridge Channel. Deep coves, shaped like bottles and retorts, can swallow up a full sized vessel, or

A little kingdom apart from the known world

fleet of vessels, like the arm of Pulpit Harbor where a fleet of steam trawlers lay rafted after the First World War, or Little River near East Boothbay where a four-masted schooner was lodged like a classic ship-in-a-bottle. In every anchorage you expected to see the clipper-bowed sloop, like a resident divinity, but almost as often you saw the small schooners, the sixty- or seventy-footers, the cargo carriers that poked in and out of six-foot channels and between voyages lay hidden and snug with bow and stern lines to the nearest trees. The coast on the outside presents a savage turmoil of breaking seas, hidden ledges, hostile lee shores, tide rips, fog banks, all the dangers of northern seas, but the change to the inner shelter of the islands can seem like a miracle. You come in on Moose Peak Light from the outside, with onshore wind, blowing fog, seas thundering on cliffs; you hear the great fog-horn blasting like doom; you see the tower like a shadow above the white breakers; you roll past into the bottle-neck of Moose Peak Channel, along the deep, deep shores of it, and suddenly all is quiet; you seem to be on a narrow lake, serenely gliding. The blasting horn is behind you; the turmoil has gone. If you desire perfect peace, more than you now have, you can work into the Mud Hole and anchor in sixteen feet of landlocked water—you can stay there a week, if you like, or forever. Nothing will bother you. You'll hear the rote of sea outside, and on quiet nights the groan of the offshore buoy—in fog you'll hear the Moose Peak horn, a comforting, half-muffled sound that enhances the stillness of your still pond.

A fine coast for pirates, but the record has very little to say about them: nor even of outlaws, in the professional sense. Men living apart are naturally anarchical; they do what they want to do. But in Maine they have kept the balance better than most—the power of evil is subdued. They mind their own business; they sometimes give way to lust or sloth, but mostly they are kind and just, and if you should be wrecked on a lonely shore they will save your life and your boat and property with no predatory intent. More, they may take you in with such good will that you are friends forever. Modern life is increasingly corrupt with the motive of profit and contempt, but some of the kindly habits persist along the coast, and if you are still lying snug in the Mud Hole a lobsterman may come in and out on his rounds and toss a couple of flipping lobsters (shorts, perhaps) into your cockpit.

The architecture of the coast is based on spruce trees, naked rock, and deep water. Other coasts in the world may be similar, but I have never seen one so well-arranged for use. The spruce gives the characteristic silhouettes, the fragrant smell of resin, and wood for fuel and building; it is good for all spars and poles, but not for fundamental boat timber such as white oak and cedar (which are also native). Hackmataek, or larch, used to be used, and white pine for decking and planking, and you once heard of green alder being bent for timbering small craft. In the classic years nearly every able-bodied man spent the good days of winter "chopping"—warming himself three times, as the old saying had it: once cutting, once loading and hauling, once burning. On clear still days they saw the smoke from burning brush like far-off neighborly signals. Much earlier, of course, great areas of forest were burned off and cleared for grazing and mowing, and many of today's thick-wooded islands were once sheep pastures; North Haven with a few of its big barns still standing was a famous place for hay and shipped off schoonerloads to mainland ports. But the forests are returning. The golden slopes of Butter Island are dark with spruce. No one wants hay; cattle are gone; sheep don't pay; the only profitable crop is the spruce itself, cut for pulp and then left to regrow in an impenetrable tangle of stumps and brush.

The rock is igneous, some of it granite of prime architectural quality: the islands south of Deer Isle, for example, seem to have been designed as formal exhibits of fine stonework, with delicate salmon-colored shades and sea-polished curves. Some cliffs and headlands are celebrated for grandeur, but even the big ones, like Monhegan's, keep within the human scale—a mere hundred and fifty feet or so, instead of the titanic heights that inspired myths and sagas. The rock of Maine is more useful than terrifying. It makes a protective breakwater at a cove's mouth, or it thrusts out from the shore like a natural wharf, or it provides a sloping plane˙ for hauling out vessels, or it takes a ringbolt to anchor a cable, or it makes a foundation for almost anything. If it were not for the islands and coves, the sea-battered coast would be as forbidding as Northern California's, but inside the outer barriers there are rocky shelters that offer comfort and security.

As cliffs are not inhumanly high, so water is not inhumanly deep. You can generally find bottom when you need to, and most natural anchorages are no more than

twenty or thirty feet. There are vaster depths everywhere
in the Aegean, or in Norway, or the Pacific-northwest,
or in the Straits of Magellan where Captain Slocum reports hauling in the anchor and fifty fathoms of cable
hanging straight up and down (I don't know that he records the weight of that anchor but I'd guess seventy
five pounds); and in Maine there are depths too—in the
fjord of Somes Sound a hundred and sixty feet, and along
the forty fathom course of the naval speed trials in West
Penobscot Bay, but in the reaches and channels a coasting
vessel could always drop anchor and wait comfortably
for a turning tide or wind.

The tides of Maine are presumed by some to be menacing, but seamen rely on them more than they fear them;
without the characteristic tides, the whole way of coastal
life would be different. East of Petit Manan tide can be
troublesome: it runs too fast and falls too far. The semi-
diurnal flow of waters east and west in and out of the
Bay of Fundy comes to seem oppressive, a sinister display
of natural power with no human relevance whatever:
even the thought of such water displacing itself, lifting
and falling with almost infinite weight and energy, day
after day through eternity, is more than mind can grasp.
To feel the whole mass of Fundy rushing inexorably, six
hours one way and six the other, can be almost frighten-
ing. We mesh our lives with the universal action of earth
and sea and all the seasons, we make use of the forces as
best we can, we base our faith and philosophy on them,
but then we have glimpses of cosmic power so vast and
inexplicable that we see ourselves carried along like the
unseen bits of plankton in that rolling flood.

But from Petit Manan westward the tides go about
their daily business more quietly. Schooners loaded in
river ports, or at the head of the long bays, waited for a
morning northerly and high water, and moved easily seaward down through the narrow channels, carried along
on the ebb. In the afternoon they brought the southerly
with them and came in on the flood—miles into the inland
reaches: you could always be surprised at the sight of a
schooner loading lumber or pulp up near the headwaters
of the Bagaduce, or far up in the inland waters of Taunton
Bay above West Sullivan. You are told that Ellsworth
was once the busiest lumber port of all, perhaps in all
the world, and you remember the shallow little channel
of the Union River and wonder how they could have
used the tides so well. And the great ships that were built
in Waldoboro and Thomaston and Wiscasset and Bath
were launched and maneuvered on the tides. At present
only yachts use sail, and nearly all the sailing yachts that
continue in and out of the rivers, or the innumerable tidal
narrows and guts, do so under power. To a modern
sailor it seems incomprehensible that a sea-going trading
brig could carry her sail right up to the wharves of
Wiscasset, twenty miles from open water. The sailing
vessels at Bangor used to be so tightly berthed, tradition
has it, that you could walk from shore to shore on their
decks. The great age of sail has become a myth, but the
men and ships did in fact perform wonders with wind and
tide.

Ten feet is the average rise for most Maine tides, and
that too is a useful arrangement. A small vessel of six-
foot draught, say, can be grounded out at high water in

the morning; by noon you can walk underneath—you can screw up a loose plank, caulk a seam, or slap on a coat of antifouling paint. You need a firm bottom, a gently sloping shore, and a wharf or rockwall for her to lean against—all fairly easily available. No one living by the shore, in and out of boats, ever forgets the time of the tides—or the nature of them. There are neap tides and spring tides, geared to the moon, and any longshore business has to reckon with them. On still, full-moon nights the flood comes in two feet or more above normal —a good time to float in a vessel if you want to haul her out; a time too when your gear floats away and vanishes forever. The lowest tides, "low dreen" you call them, seem a little sinister, and reveal hidden bottoms and old bones you didn't know were there—all black and weedy with undersea mystery; but it is the right time to find lost moorings and anchors, or to go and dig for seaclams. You can't really visualize a coast where there is no movement of waters on the shores, no beds of seaweed, no clam flats, no mussels. You wonder how people on a tideless sea lift and move great weights—you remember the times you have slung a ton mooring stone under two boats and waited for the slow but inexorable lift, or perhaps the very critical times you have gone aground, fetched up hard and solid on a ledge, and summoned up all your reserves of patience and faith until the flood carried you off. Perhaps you think of the creatures that enjoy the tidal shores, the seals asleep on weedy ledges, the gulls and fish crows poking about for edible shellfish: you may even relish the smell of flats and barnacled rocks and wet seaweed—a strong and heady sea-smell, as people call it, which other coasts, such as California's, don't have.

In older times, when all travel was by sea, the islands were bound more closely to one another and the main. The highroads were the ship channels, but innumerable byroads led in and out, the little thoroughfares, narrows, guts, where local sloops and dories and peapods became a modest sort of traffic. "Local knowledge" was needed for navigation, and strangers hired pilots—expert in their own region but perhaps ignorant about others: one early cruiser reported hiring a man to take his vessel across the bar between Deer Isle and Little Deer, and they ran hard aground. A not unusual event in that spot, I should add. Today a state road blocks it, and few realize that once the main traffic flowed across it the other way.

There is hardly an island of any size in Maine without traces of old habitation—the cellar, the filled-in well, the walls for penning sheep and cattle, the remnant of wharf. What is now a thick stand of spruce used to be a dooryard, a potato and bean patch, a mowing for hay, and a great cropped pasture for sheep. Some of the old farm places still remain, preserved by summer people: you see the beautiful house on Leadbetter's Island and think what dignity and peace such a life must have had—and the community on Roque Island, or Bartlett's Island, how idyllic they seem on a summer day with their clapboard houses and green mowings. You think in places like that existence must have reached an ideal balance of serenity and labor and natural felicity; you think of *The Country of the Pointed Firs*, and Green Island, and that end-product of a perfect civilization, Mrs. Blackett, living with her middle-aged son William in a kind of classic purity and finality, like the figures on an urn.

I remember that life, especially in Penobscot Bay: the old yellow farmhouse on Butter Island that tried to turn itself into a resort called Dirigo, now wholly deserted and growing up to spruce—I used to hear of the scythe-swingers who went to mow the great hay fields of Butter. All that's left is a gravestone, lost in alders and spruce. I recollect the remnants of the house on Bradbury Island, and the well, and the cleared land, and the far view down the bay, now all an impenetrable jungle. There were houses on Pickering (one haunted), a fine place on Hog (lately restored), a grave of a man named John Walton on Great Spruce Head (still so far as I know unidentified in our world), and best of all a little community on Eagle, with school, post office, lighthouse, and at one time steamer service to Rockland. As of now, two inhabitants remain to Eagle, faithful to its old demands, with horse, cow, sheep, and cats, but no boat; the school has been empty for a generation, the lighthouse is automatic, but some trickle of life still comes and goes in summer along with a sort of vestigial mail service held over from a more prosperous past.

The larger and better-known outer islands, Monhegan, Matinicus, and Criehaven, Isle au Haut, Frenchboro (Lunt's as it used to be, Outer Long as it is on the charts), maintain their communities with traditional pride and some contempt for all outsiders and landsmen. They feel abandoned and neglected by the politicians on the main; in their hearts they know they are dwindling—each year they count fewer schoolchildren; their fate depends on lobsters and herring, and they haven't too much faith in either—

not in the long run, that is; but they are loyal to their
generations, they are full of pride and vanity at their
competence at sea and ashore, and they love the freedom
of their lives. They are conscious of the long past behind
them, a century—even two centuries on their outposts;
they remember fathers and grandfathers, and their linked
chain of memory sometimes goes backward to the old
sea battle of the War of 1812, or the grim year of 1816
when there was no summer, and to some of the wrecks
and disasters of old times. There seems to be no place on
earth too hard for men to inhabit, or too remote or meager
in resources, and often the very hardness gives a drama
they come to relish. A man commanding a small boat on a
winter sea can at least be proud of himself and happy to
come home to warmth and safety. He knows where he
lives and what he must do. He knows who he is.

Of all the little sea kingdoms of the coast the mellow-
est, most prosperous, and the farthest from the main, is
Matinicus, which seems to retain its vitality in spite of the
modern changes. Good lobstering keeps them going there,
plus a deep-rooted loyalty and love. It is not a rocky outpost of fishermen's shacks and wharves, but rather a gentle
little country of meadows and gardens and white-painted
clapboard houses with doorways of old New England
grace. There are formal parlors and family Bibles and the
sacred bits of good china and furnishings passed on from
early times, along with treasures touched by the romance
of the wrecks of long ago. There is a well-tended country
cemetery, with stones marking the life and death of generations of Youngs and Ameses and the other royal lines
of the island. There used to be cattle, mowings, plowed

land, and a network of little roads and paths with barred gates and stiles—now all changed, with automobiles on the roads, and milk and fresh food sent by the mailboat from Rockland. But nowhere on the coast do you feel more vividly the evanescent past, the old self-sufficiency of a world of the oar and sail, of the ax and saw, of life sustained by farming and fishing and the work done by hand. On the high meadow on the southern, sea-facing end of the island stands one of the loveliest little farm places in the country, a white clapboard house with the classic doorways and moldings, a barn, shade trees, flowers brighter and fresher than mainland flowers, and all round are the buttery green summer meadows, full of daisies and hawkweed, all rank and uncut now, sweeping off toward the sea. Wherever you look, in the whole circumference, you have glimpses of the sea like a great bowl of blue light. And the horizon line is always level, always straight, always there, like an assertion of pure logical truth.

A sentiment for the old world and its ways is inescapable for anyone who can remember them. You talk yourself out of it; you argue that nostalgia is the last refuge of the coward; you puncture illusion and adopt the tough-minded view; but if you are of a certain age and habit, you succumb. No one now living who used to take the steamer from Boston to Rockland can ever forget it, or speak of it or think of it without a little tightening of the throat. The Bangor Boat, they called it. It ran every day—and "it" was one of two ships, earlier the side-wheelers the *City of Bangor* and the *City of Rockland*, later the turbines *Camden* and *Belfast*: one left Boston, the other left Bangor, in late afternoon—they must have passed off Casco Bay somewhere, though I was never awake to see. In winter they reduced the schedule to two or three round trips a week. But to every normal passenger, young or old, the voyage from Boston had a celestial feeling about it, as though one were being translated from the dust and heat of earth to the threshold of heaven. To the ship and her crew it was all part of a daily and perhaps monotonous routine, but the sense of anticipation was electric in the air and when the ship trembled with its power and voices cried out orders and warnings, and the whistle shattered your very soul, and the solid wharf and city began to move, slip away backward, you knew that one of your life's great voyages had begun; you ran out to be in the wind, forward on the upper deck, you felt released from dust and turmoil of city, you saw ships, lighters, tugs, barges, schooners—a Banks fisherman in the main channel, coming toward you wing and wing with the afternoon southeasterly; you passed a flashing buoy, heard the clang of a bell, saw the sun on the whitewashed tower of Boston Light, you tasted the cold of the wind, and then you felt the slow long heave and swing of the open sea, the tremble of the great ship as she rolled to port, slowly, slowly, surging down and down, then slowly coming to a pause, almost with a vast sigh, and slowly again lifting herself for the long, long starboard roll as though she were keeping time to some cosmic rhythm too vast for mortal senses. Then the sunset over Cape Ann, dust-red above the hot land, and the twin lights of Thatcher's Island clear in the dusk, and after that if you stayed out bravely in the cold air you'd see the pin-point gleam of the Isles of Shoals.

Then the nightlong rush and surge of the ship, the beat of engines, the tremble and shudder of the whole fabric, the stateroom turning colder and colder until you shivered under the thin cotton blanket, and at last you woke suddenly to daylight and knew that you had come through the zone and barrier between two worlds. You were there. You dressed fast with sweater and coat and broke out of your cell, out into the icy air of a Maine morning. You smelled it first, the spruce, the fir—you breathed it. Smell of wet ledges too, seaweed, kelp. You paced the wet decks—everything was beaded and sparkling with wet; you faced the ship's wind and thought of icebergs somewhere offshore, though you saw by the silvery-blue sheen of the waters that there was no real wind. And right off the port beam was an island, wooded, dark, green, laced with surf along its rock faces—Monroe Island. It looked pure in the dawn light, and a flicker of gold seemed to touch its tree tops—sun was coming, you realized. No one in sight—the island seemed to be perfectly pristine, as though it were on exhibition as a sample of Maine coast creation. The breakers creaming along its cliffs caught some of the gold of sunrise. You passed very close to a bell buoy—all you could hear of it was a harsh clank as it pitched in the ship's wash. She turned; you saw Owl's Head Light, the tower pure white now in the sun, and there before you the harbor of Rockland opened, and the great schooners lying at anchor, pointing southward, masts and lofty bowsprits gleaming, some with mizzens or spankers set, all as still as a dream vision.

It was a colder and brighter and cleaner world than the one you left yesterday. Forested mountains stretched

Great schooners lying at anchor pointing southward, masts and
lofty bowsprits gleaming, some with mizzens or spankers set,
all as still as a dream vision

northward, and as far as you could see up the wide bay
northeastward and eastward were the islands and channels full of the mystery of loneliness and distance. The air
was still cold in your throat and lungs, the smell of shore
and forest promised such beauty and delight as you had
never known. A new world, you thought.

An illusion, a dream—but everyone who came there
shared it, the young ones full of the hope of a long golden
summer, the old ones returning from voyages, strangers,
and natives all felt it. A world not only of islands and
waterways and forests and headlands, but of people with
habits and voices and characters different from those elsewhere. You could hear the voices right away on the Rockland wharf—someone calling the name Bar Harbor in the
accents of a lost sheep or Stonington without the letter
"g," or Eggemoggin as though it began with "aidge." You
could hear bits of anecdote: "Why she come into that
wharf just like an ax into an egg box. . . ." Talk, voices,
people, and the domain of salt water. Little steamers in all
directions. Life in the harbor, tugs moving, sails hoisting
with the echoing creak of double blocks, white-winged
gulls planing in the blue overhead, day warming and bur-
geoning—and now you are off again in an island steamer,
the *Pemaquid* or the *J. T. Morse*, with a long blast of
whistle and powerful churning of paddle wheels, heading
east again into the islanded region that seems to you the
ultimate realm of gold.

It exists still, of course; the elementals are there, the
islands, forested shores, cold sea and cold wind, and the
little harbors, the white villages, the people, voices, but
the unique quality of separateness is no longer there. The

places once remote and alone are now part of the world: airplanes come and go, and fast power boats and automobiles. Television, of course. Highways by land and air. The universal mechanics of modern life.

TWO

PEOPLE

And of all the foure parts of the world that I
have yet seene not inhabited, could I have but
meanes to transport a Colonie, I would rather live
here than any where: and if it did not maintaine it
selfe, were wee but once indifferently well fitted,
let us starve.

Captain John Smith

A PLACE TOO HARSH destroys the humanity man is
capable of. Darwin reports on the bestiality of
the people of Tierra del Fuego, who lived naked
in the wind-driven sleet and in desperation devoured their
old women. At the other extreme the legend of Eden implies that ease and comfort also destroy. Mankind is generally in the middle somewhere, between hot and cold,
dry and wet, mountain and plain, sea and shore, beast and
god. The cold tempers and whets his character, the
warmth gives him rest and idle dreams.

Maine is on the northern fringe, and endures long and
hard winters—still hard even in our time of efficient heat
and mobility. But the peoples of those northern zones
have strength: the Russians, Scandinavians, Scots—all
tending to be dour, more or less gloomy, but physically
and morally formidable. So with the northern New Englanders, mostly of English and Scottish origin but shaped

for two and even three centuries by the somewhat harsher
country of their new world. They made a victory out of
their survival. They coped with deep snow and thirty-
below-zero temperatures, with rough country, forests,
rocky land, isolation. And then in late spring, in early May,
they burgeoned and blossomed into a region of wondrous
beauty and delight. For those five or six months, the
northern world is as temperate and fair as any known to
man, and the land was rich in milk and honey and all other
produce.

Perhaps the coast differs in some ways. Sea winds
blow harder than inland winds. Cold is less intense, but at
times more penetrating. Spring comes more slowly. Sea
work is more dangerous than land work. But in compensa-
tion the coastal summer may be sweeter, balmier, altogether more delightful than any summer anywhere on
earth.

Out of all this, of course, came moral strength and
self-reliance. But other qualities can be noticed. An almost classless society, for one thing: every person was
what he was, with an equal claim on the respect of all. He
was recognized for what he could be and do. Some rose
in esteem, became select by virtue of ability; others sank
and lived on the town. But they were all members of the
community—which actually operated like a big family.
Everyone addressed everyone else, old or young, rich or
poor, by first name or nickname: children called out to the
judge in his buggy "Hi, *Challie!*"—assuming his name to
be Charles Howard or Spofford or Clifford. Everyone
tended to be related to everyone else, and the shipmaster
on King Row might be cousin to the town charges in their

tar-paper shack on Fish Creek. And with all this network
of kinship there was more affection than hostility. Isolation often breeds hatred, and families and neighbors nour-
ish hereditary feuds—not here the murderous shooting
feuds of Corsica or Kentucky, but frequently the repressed
inner hatreds that afflict responsible citizens like a con-
tagious insanity. But far more potent than the hatred
is the affection and compassion that hovers over the Maine
community, the anxious responsibility for the welfare of
everyone, the neighborly generosity and service, the tele-
phoning and inquiring, the carrying of food or fuel, the
digging out of drifts or cutting away trees after a storm.
The old tradition of mutual help on land or sea is strong:
any man with a boat holds himself ready for search or
rescue, night or day. Death or disaster to anyone is a
poignant grief to all.

The democratic and communal habit has little theoretical or self-conscious basis; it exists as the natural outcome
of old conditions. Some of it is based simply on good
character, or on what the moral anarchists of our time
would condemn as puritanism—assuming that any stern
ethical code is an evil; actually the early puritan rigors of
the Boston region never controlled the people of Maine,
whose codes were firm and practical rather than doctrinal
and tinged with madness. They lived, the down-easters,
in a state of mutual respect and coöperation partly because
they were good people to begin with, and partly because
the pioneer work of settling, cutting forests, clearing land,
building and using boats, could be better done with communal good will. The life was not suited to an idle gentry; wealth was moderate at best, and what really counted

was competence. It is always said that the old town-meeting political system of New England represented the purest form of practical democracy—a system no longer suited to our complicated world, as the authorities now tell us. But where all were equal and known, and unconstrained by arbitrary power or fear or serious grievance, pure democracy flourished naturally and even inevitably, without need of indoctrination. A man with his own farm, houses, livestock, with a hundred acres of pasture and forest, with his fleet of boats for fishing or trading, was as free and as equal as a man could be. He had little need to be covetous or angry at fate or his neighbors or his governors. If in the end he failed, went bankrupt, took to drink, the blame, he would admit, was largely his own.

An idyllic episode in the long and tragic history of man, but true—as many have testified and as a few can still remember. New country, good people, space, freedom, challenge: the conditions may never again exist on earth.

But as to character itself, what can be said? The "goodness" existed among them as a code, as it did among all the New England pioneers: it was based on an unquestioned belief in Christian ethics and the omnipotence of God. Discipline and repression were part of it, and may have induced evils such as self-righteousness and bigotry: present-day philosophers would like to think so, at least. But as far as the conditions of their lives permitted they achieved a steadier happiness than our age of enlightened anxiety can discover for itself. The hardships were often severe, the storms and disasters, the sickness and early death, and certainly spiritual misery is the common lot

anywhere, but their vocation and their faith kept them so
fully occupied that they had no time to question their
destiny. Here they were, here was the work to be done,
here were the rules: a grim life for many, perhaps, but one
worth the living. A man could win victories, small or
large, over land or sea, against the weather and the natural
properties he handled; he could take pride in his mastery.
A woman, whose labor was longer and often harder, had
the vision of family strength and support; she linked generation to generation in a great chain.

Were such people dour? hard-bitten? dry? reticent?
Were they the Yankees of books and plays? sexually repressed? lustful, like characters in O'Neill? or perhaps
cracker-barrel humorists and salt-water philosophers?
After much of a lifetime among them I find that no category is adequate. Perhaps a week's visit would make judgment simpler: the summer tourist in France knows more
about the French than the life-long inhabitant. But wary
observers come to feel more and more that men everywhere are what they are, and mostly share the given traits
of Homo sapiens. The visible part of behavior reflects the
manners and customs, and the clothes and houses and ges-
tures that may or may not reveal the psyche underneath.
A "foreigner," an Italian stonecutter, say, settled in Maine
for a couple of decades, takes on the local look and manner, and his children are hardly distinguishable from their
native fellows: they even learn the rhythms and percus-
sions of speech that seem so incomprehensible to outsiders.

But yet, if you allow endless exceptions, there are traits
that go deep into the region of soul. In her life of Char-
lotte Brontë, Elizabeth Gaskell very sharply and strongly

defines the Yorkshire character: they are a *hard* people, she says; they are suspicious, tenacious, fiercely individualistic, implacable enemies, and warm friends. Whether she is right I can't say, but one is tempted to see a similar toughness in the Maine people. Not that fierceness is characteristic of them—rather they are more gentle and affectionate than most. But they are strong and resolute, they keep their emotions under severe control, they speak in understatements, they are wary of outsiders. They clearly perceive the virtues of their own tradition, perhaps sometimes they are complacent about it: they remember the good deeds of their fathers and grandfathers, the honorable successes of able seamen and captains. They admire competence, of course, and expect it of all worthy men. And they expect courtesy too; it is part of that long tradition that has come from their seafaring past, the slightly formal protocol that belongs to ships and their conduct in the great world. On one level they seem to have lived a localized and provincial life, with country dialect and quaint occupations; on another, they reflect almost a courtliness, a traditional dignity that belongs to large visions and enterprises.

It is vanishing, the old folk think. The young take their manners from the vulgarities of popular entertainment. Courtesy exists only incidentally, as an easy and flippant surface manner; it masks the indifference below. The complaint is universal in our time: the good old ways pass, vulgarization comes in. A vast social leveling goes on: the good is pulled down, but perhaps some of the bad is raised. In earlier Maine there was more good than bad.

But I suppose the bad existed and deserves notice.

When robberies used to occur, when houses were looted of blankets, or equipment and boats were stolen, the culprits were presumed to be "men in schooners"—who could come ashore in darkness and do bad things. One community always blamed another. Vinal Haven knew it was the Deer Islanders who did it. Deer Isle blamed it on Little Deer Isle. But in this day of incessant major crime, those depredations seem small. There were poachings, lobster wars, fierce local hatreds leading to violence—there still are. I have seen angry young men attacking a lobsterman's lonely outpost on an island, breaking up his gear, and throwing his traps into the sea: doubtless they were full of self-righteousness in their own cause.

Perhaps these are only surface evils. What of the warped souls, the sexual perversions and repressions? A diligent Freudian can find them anywhere—and everywhere—but in actuality the old coastal Yankees got through their sexual ordeals quite comfortably. The institution of marriage worked better than it does now, but of course required greater restraint and loyalty and less self-indulgence. No doubt some were injured or even destroyed by sexual fear and hypocrisy, and there was more illegitimacy than was ever admitted. One must separate rumor and fiction from what one actually knows. My experience has been mainly with a people whose desire was to be loyal and affectionate and conscientious, and who were willing to subdue (or repress) their personal yearnings. If the Freudian stipulates that such repression leads inevitably to misery and deformity I can say only that I think he is wrong: at least he is wrong to build a dogma on it. An old French medal of honor has the words *valeur et discipline* on it, which I suppose have to do with the behavior of soldiers, but it might be bestowed on anyone who can make decent order out of the chaos of reality.

And nothing gives a man more moral support than competence. If he can handle a situation he can be happy, and in the old coastal time there was almost no problem that a good man couldn't master. Farmer and fisherman were just the beginning: carpenter, mason, smith, rigger —anything a man could do with hands and tools he could do. A man and an ox between them could haul a vessel up into a field, or move a house, or raise a barn. In the winter he cut cordwood or pulpwood or saw logs and toted them to a mill or a vessel for loading. In spring he plowed and planted, and caulked and painted and launched his boats. He sheared his sheep and put them off to pasture —sometimes on the wild islands. He set out a fish weir; he tarred his nets. All summer he fished and farmed—got in his hay, sailed his clams or his fresh herring or salt mackerel to market or factory, harvested his vegetables and berries for canning, and his potatoes and apples, brought home his sheep, slaughtered a few critters for meat and fat in the cold weather, repaired his fences and buildings, hauled out his boats, sharpened his axes for the winter chopping. All this is merely a faint outline of the realities. His wife had more to do, with washing and mending and preserving and cooking and lugging wood and water and tending chickens and making soap and butter and lard and raising children and healing the sick. Those who survived did well, and were strong and sometimes happy; others perished.

It seems often that the true mark of the down-east
character is its humor, and certainly humor is indigenous;
but it may be hard to define it as a special characteristic.
All good people—perhaps one should say all civilized
people—have humor, but between childish nonsense on
the one hand and philosophical irony on the other the
range is too wide to be included under a single label.
Yankee humor, as everyone knows, is pretty much a philosophical irony. It accepts the facts of life with a quiet
and somewhat fatalistic detachment. It perceives how the
facts contradict the hopes and intentions that accompany
them. Out of the paradox a new fact emerges, which is the
inevitable absurdity that a man must cope with. And these
perceptions are so woven into the fabric of life that they
exist as a sort of ancient wisdom rather than as a discovery
or a source of drama or emotion. The Yankee is not likely
to laugh aloud, or to weep, or to curse God. It is as
though he knew all along that he is lucky to get on as well
as he does in the face of the implacable powers of nature,
and if he can score a small victory here or there, outwit a
storm at sea, survive a cold winter, he is doing better than
he might expect. He knows that failure would be more in
accord with the normal realities, the small hopes of man
pitted against the nonhuman forces. Somewhere in the back
of his consciousness he believes that God is on his side, and
that the long struggle of life does avail him something,
both here and hereafter, but meanwhile he is thankful for
whatever good luck occurs, and is aware of the natural
prevalence of bad luck.

It is this kind of irony that gives the particular wrinkles
and gleams about his eyes, the little twist to the corners of

his mouth, but mainly sounds in the dry accents of his voice. "They come down over them jagged rocks on the quarry road," one will say, carrying along a story, "and blew out all four tires at once." And a quiet voice will say, "Good shot." But no writing can convey the implications in the sound of those two small words; each one can evoke the whole folly and absurdity of the human predicament. The quality of the voice tones, the dry relish of the vowel sounds, the finality of the little words, specially the second, produce a perfect little comic drama. There we all are together, by God. A bunch of damn fools on a quarry road with four flat tires. Good shot!

In Maine the accent is everything. Listen to the tones, the way the words are said, and you hear the sound of irony, acceptance, folly, tough-mindedness. "I looked down and saw them barnacles right under me, I was some scairt." "You scrape bottom on 'em?" "Well, we didn't strike, but it took the hide off o' *my* bottom, I tell you."

I recollect a small scene at a village post office where the rickety flagstaff and the flag had carried away, and the postmaster was somewhat tangled up in the attempt to straighten them. "What's Washington goin' to do when they hear about this?"—from a bystander. And the quick response by the postmaster: "You won't tell 'em, will you?"

The accent is so turned to humor that the outsider often can't tell what is serious and what isn't. The solemn man speaks in the same tones and rhythms as the humorous man, and it takes experience to distinguish them: the difference between an insult and a jest is not a smile, but an implication detected only by a trained ear. In a small scene in *The Country of the Pointed Firs*, a man on a wharf is calling advice to Almira Todd about how to handle a dory —and she turns "with some difficulty" to see who it is: "That you, Asa? Good mornin'. . . . When'd you git back from up country?" It is stipulated that she spoke politely, but Asa and the other onlookers recognized the implications. Part of the old Yankee code is that everyone knows how to do what he is doing; you don't give advice unless you are asked to, and if you find it necessary to be critical of someone, or ironic, you do it with such quiet tact that you seem not to be doing it at all.

The language of humor in Maine is said to be picturesque, or "colorful," but that is probably a literary assumption. The Mississippi raftsmen of Mark Twain may be somewhat literary too, but they indulge in the kind of picturesque eloquence that has no echo in northern New England. Tall stories, exaggerations, extravagances, belong to other areas.

The character of the "old-timer" in Maine is well known, perhaps so familiar as to seem to be a cliché, yet he does still exist as an unforgettable reality. We know him in actuality, and we know that some of his good characteristics derived from his old-fashioned ways. He was brought up in sail, and learned patience. And he learned how to deal at first hand with the vast natural force of wind and water. His motion was part of the larger motions of the visible world he lived in, and whenever he hoisted the double-block tackle of a throat halyard, or got in chain link by link on a hand windlass, he was making direct use of the kind of power that seemed native to him. What he achieved was control rather than speed, a slow but sure joining of all available forces. Patience—and an almost intuitive rapport with his surroundings. In the years of his survival he lost the cockiness and vanity other men have, nor did he adopt a pose of humility: he simply did what he did with full knowledge of the hazards and responsibilities, with confidence in his ability, with an almost fatalistic acceptance of the natural conditions. He was slow to criticize others for folly or failure—he knew that trouble at sea afflicted even the most competent.

At home, among people, he behaved with a gentle courtliness that now seems part of another world. The deep-water men of the last century, specially the officers, assumed that good manners were part of their professions. A captain in port wore a stovepipe hat and a frock coat and addressed his mate as mister. Long, long ago, that seems, yet the old habits persisted in later generations of coastwise sailors: the old-timer is still remembered as a courteous and kindly man who had somehow achieved serenity of soul.

THREE

THE WAYS
OF LIFE

> Here every man may be master and owner of
> his own labour and land, or the greatest part in a
> small time.
> ... Yet the Sea there is the strangest fishpond
> I ever saw; and those barren Iles so furnished
> with good woods, springs, fruits, fish, and foule, that
> it make me thinke, though the Coast be Rockie,
> and this affrightable; the Vallies, Plaines, and
> interior parts may well (notwithstanding) be very
> fertile.
>
> *Captain John Smith*

SELF-SUFFICIENCY is a state of mind still possible along
the coast, but the practice dwindles. Carpenters and
plumbers do work for summer people, and thrive,
but a house may now be contracted for in Bangor, say,
and trucked down and set up by a crew of strangers;
wells are drilled by a huge automatic apparatus that can
travel from afar; boats are factory-built of metal or glass.
The old ways of fishing are impractical, and even a new
Maine-built trawler costing several hundred thousand is
said to be inadequate compared with steel ships such as
Russia builds.

The only continuing one-man, one-boat industry is

lobstering, and so far the corporations have not taken charge of it. Rumors fly, fear grows, of course: deep-water vessels now drag for lobsters far offshore, and may, it is said, upset the old cycles of breeding and distribution. And from York to Cutler so much lobstering is done it seems a wonder any are left: yet year after year the supply holds, and cargoes are trucked off to cities. Larger pounds are built, larger operations; but the essential element is still the man who goes out to haul his traps. He does it alone, or with one companion, and his gear is very like his grandfather's.

New traps are invented, new materials and shapes, but the classic model of laths and bent saplings remains the standard—perhaps with cement slab for weight instead of flat rocks, and with nylon twine for the nets. The long line to the buoy, the "pot warp," could be nylon too, but is more likely to be treated sisal, which is cheaper (honest old manilla hemp seems to be disappearing from rope stores). Toggles and buoys are mostly the long-used bottles and shaped rounds of pine (now mass produced), but air-blown plastic that floats like a bubble is more and more frequent.

But the methods remain. A chunk of bait, old herring or any old fish, is stuffed in a net bag and fixed inside the little prison of the trap, which is dropped overboard at the chosen spot, and sinks to the bottom—and of course the victim works its way through to the point of no return; crabs do too, and other shelly creatures and now and then a genuine fish. In a day or two the fisherman returns, hooks up his buoys and warp, winds it on the little winch connected to his motor, and lets it come in—a dextrous

The only continuing one-man, one-boat industry

maneuver that involves the positioning of the boat, the control of the motor, the handling of a lot of line which knots and snarls to the best of its ability, and the hauling out of the trap—heavy now with water and whatever else it may hold.

He works generally alone, and his chosen spot may be among remote ledges or shoals, or off a lee shore with heavy sea breaking. He may be cautious about fog and storm, but once he is out on his grounds he takes his chances as they come. He may be far off, an hour's run from harbor. He may have troubles, a dead motor, a bent propeller, or he may catch a hand in the turning drum of his winch, or lurch overboard as he reaches for the weighted trap: all such things happen; and now and then a boat is found drifting empty. Perhaps he has a ship-to-shore radio telephone, as many do—perhaps it is the one thing that saves him in trouble. But his day's work is all part of the old way of a man dealing at firsthand with the primitive realities. Perhaps there is something about the lobster itself, the most primeval of all creatures, that requires such a solitary and venturesome operation. Perhaps the lone fisherman reflects on the irony of a life devoted to the trials and hazards of capturing and sending such improbable monsters off to market for the pleasure of the rich and idle, as he may think.

But as long as his income is more than his outgo, he lives well and is not envious of others. His well-being is the old-time well-being of the man who is on his own. In the dawn, at four o'clock, he is up because he decides to be; he walks down his own path to his own piece of shore, hauls in the punt he himself built, rows off to what he takes more pride in than any other object in his life—his powerboat, his long high-bowed beauty with her great flair forward and deep sheer and straight run aft and wide stern. He might have built her himself, many do, but more likely he had her built from a model he approved—a Jonesport model, perhaps; the best, fastest, handsomest lobster boats on all the coast come from Jonesport. More power in her than he really needs, of course, but power is pride and delight: if he is still young and full of vanity he drives her at twenty knots or even more, and shows off her paces in rough water. The old, the conservative, are content with twelve or fourteen knots, but even that demands up-to-date power and more gallons of fuel than they wish they had to buy.

Seining for herring has been a four- or five-man operation, at times profitable. A true gamble, they say. A fleet is needed, dories, seine boats, small and large powerboats, and in these times a plane to find and follow schools of fish from the air above. Money can be made in a good season, or lost in a bad one, and the good and bad are controlled by many variables: when herring are plentiful and sardines are in demand, small fortunes are made, but this collaboration is becoming rare. The herring are more likely to be stored in hogsheads and sold for lobster bait. An old-time feature of the coast was the small canning factory—for sardines, or clams or crabs: from Lubec to Portland there were many plants, mostly quite small, now one by one disappearing. Perhaps the Maine sardine is taken as a subsistence ration, not suitable for the affluence of our society. The lobster flourishes and the sardine dwindles. As for other fish, they seem to dwindle too, both

A Jonesport model, perhaps

in fact and esteem. Their value for sport may rise, but for commerce it seems to decline.

Maine is described by geologists as a sinking coast line, which may be the cause of its beauty. The islands are old mountain peaks. But the motive of sinking runs through its physical and spiritual life: no one can be there without strongly feeling that things aren't what they used to be, and actually and truthfully aren't as good as they used to be. It is a fundamental New England illusion, and can be shown to be true or false as the arguer pleases. Change generally seems tragic, and perhaps is: one of the solemn concepts of modern physics is that all matter wastes itself and is consumed by time. Whatever may come— however old things reconstitute themselves—the simple fact is that once a balance of nature, both human and non-human, existed along the coast, and now no longer exists. The remnants of it show like the island peaks, symbols of submerged ranges—even the hulls of noble wooden ships here and there, and houses like classic remains, and village streets, and mostly the old people with their manners from another century and their long, long memories. The new ships are emblems of power, and are linked to General Motors or one of the other great producers of engines, and the houses seem to have been conceived and executed by some manufacturer of what are called mobile homes. The economy depends mostly on the money brought in by vacationers.

Once or perhaps twice in the past the region prospered well: the first was the great lumber period, when the Penobscot and other rivers were paved with golden sawdust and the wood of inland Maine, white pine, was shipped all over the western world—part, actually, of the classic great days of New England trade. What remains to us is a vision of beautiful white houses and all that we now admire as antiques, with families of great respectability whom we can claim as our forebears, but what made it all possible in its time was great profit. The enterprise was vigorous—and free.

The salt-fish period was much less prosperous, but it provided a working economy for the small harbors of the coast. Fish once lived in great plenty in the Maine waters, as Captain John Smith and others testified—so much so that vessels came from England to catch and salt them years before the Pilgrims landed: and even into this century the old ways of hand-lining and gang-trawling were profitable, and the local sloops and schooners flourished. The village of South Deer Isle is seen as a scatter of small houses along the highway, with a stretch of empty, sheltered water on one side, a tidal cove on the other—no store, no post office, probably no people in sight. A few of the white houses are quite perfect models of the simplest classic period, and at once strike you as beautiful and pure, with shade trees and a few flowers about. But the village—it hardly seems to deserve even that title—has no visible reason to exist: no farms, no boats, no tourist attractions. The traveler has no way of knowing that it grew up after the Civil War as a fishing port, famous on the coast, with chandleries, customs house, salt supply, and a fleet of vessels. All gone, except for the half-dozen pretty houses. In some parts of the world the relics remain forever, preserved in dry air or protected by stone, but the wood-built civilization of New England can be lost in a few decades.

Two men between them can remember a century. My father remembered the death of Lincoln, and that his father wept. There are still a few who knew Sarah Orne Jewett who wrote about the decline of the great days of Maine even as early as the 1870's: was she beguiled by nostalgia and the thought of the earlier glories of her own family? Did she have a sort of literary dream of a golden age? She wrote a story called "All My Sad Captains," and the title sounds like a knell for old Maine. She alluded always to the old ways, the old manners, as though she were writing a valedictory: once, long ago, there were heroes and heroines; they sailed the Seven Seas; they lived up to a formal code of honor and kindliness and competence; their names were Blackett and Bowden and Littlepage; they were all old—it seems in a way that they must have been always old, always looking back to a time of greatness. It was an Indian summer mood, and has continued for almost a century—fading away at last in the face of overwhelming change, but still felt by anyone over fifty. Even now on the coast a few sailing captains linger on as symbols of an era that seems indistinguishable from myth and legend.

And the little salt-water farms are there, too, the houses and barns, at least, taken over by summer people or retired city people and still visibly representing the security and peace of the old life. A clapboard house, story-and-a-half as they say, with shingled outhouse, woodsheds, chicken house, icehouse, sheep pen, cow barn, and hayloft all surrounding in linked defense against wind and weather, well back from the shore and away from the open waters, looking down over green meadows and gray ledges to a land-

ing with boat shop, ways, moorings, sea relics of all kinds.
A self-contained world. Marketable sheep, with wool and
meat for home use. A milch cow or two, a beef critter,
a pig, hens, a horse for traveling by buggy, oxen for power
—all normal equipment on a one-family farm. The largest
crop would be hay, the next potatoes, then beans. Rhubarb
behind the woodshed. A scatter of apple trees. Wild berries
in the pastures. Cords of spruce wood, cut in the woodlot
in winter, hauled in by ox sled, sawed, split, and stacked by
hand, a steady cold-weather operation. All this was the
pattern of any working farm, but these were also seamen.
They fished offshore, carried cargoes in schooners, built
and maintained their vessels, hauled them and launched
them with oxen, cut the spars in their woods, shaped and
bent the iron in their forge. They salted and dried cod and
haddock, set up a weir for mackerel and herring, caught
flounders on hook and line in the channel of the cove or
speared them in shallow waters at night with torches for
light. And infinite clams always available, for home or
market or factory.

The generations could come and go on such a place
without much aid or comfort from the outside world, with
no threat of famine or blight. All the necessaries were
available. Life could be, in the traditional way, idyllic.
Even the beauty contributed, and the natural purity of all
the great elements, the sea and forest and air. There was
kindliness, self-respect, a competence that seemed able to
cope with every crisis or demand: the Fox Islanders, an
old record says, were "noted for their humanity and
benevolence to strangers."

But the record must also admit that man's grasp is not

anywhere near as good as his reach. Many lovely old domains did exist, you can see them, the houses and barns
and meadows and shores and sheltered waters; they were
actually created and managed. But from report and memory you know that human nature was not always strong
enough to cope with them. It took a stout body and soul
to keep it all going from light to dark every day for a
lifetime. If a man paused long enough to take stock, he
probably reckoned his tasks somewhat like this: roof to re-
shingle, gutters rotten, paint in poor shape, pasture fence
about gone, alders crowding in, blade on mower busted,
wheel off the rake, horse seems to have colic, off ox is
lame, hay still wet—needs turning—pond dry, dam broken
somewhere, weeds in the beans, corn pretty pindling, rust
in the pump water—or is it mud? And the boats—dory in
the sun there, drying out, sloop leaking in the rudder port
—should be hauled out, ought to lift the mooring too—
can't trust it any more. Mackerel coming in good, they
say—but the weir's all gone to hell. Could sell clams if
there was any time to dig a bushel or two. . . . And all this
is only the obvious daily demand, a sort of basic tally of
the facts of life. It is possible to imagine the special problems, the aches and pains, the ailing wife, the minor
plagues, the irresponsible children, the human frailties of
all ages.

The gospel of work is a fine one in a world of strong
and capable people, but when work is too much and bodies
too weak, desperation may result. Or simply defeat, or
resignation, or the imperceptible sinking and letting go.
The farm places could crumble away in rot and litter,
and many did, even in the good old days. Perhaps it was

the woman who held them together, those strong characters recorded so often in literature, dedicated wholly to cleanliness and godliness: Mrs. Blackett at the age of eighty-six turned the best-room carpet—beat it and swept it on the grass and resewed it—an act of supreme virtue and faith, and even now many can remember the women of that moral and spiritual strength who lived up to their own stern visions. Many remember what often happened in the houses without good women, the piling up of dirt and confusion, the proliferation of cats, the squirrels in the attic and vermin in the bedding, the peeling wall paper, the burlap sacking in the broken window, the stink of bad air and mildew in closed rooms.

Life in the northeastern coast has been thought to be too wintry and hard for the best kind of culture. All efforts go into survival in the year-round war with cold weather. If culture embodies the making of great art, perhaps there is truth in the argument—or was in the days when survival in the cold north was less easy than it may be now. But moral and psychological strength may be the basis of great culture, and northern peoples have done better at it than those in more temperate places. They did actually achieve a dignity and competence in life, which is a measure of what we call civilization. For those who could cope with it, the harsh challenge of the old northern coast, on both land and sea, produced moral and physical strength, and, beyond that, spiritual serenity.

FOUR

TALK

"She's seen all the trouble folks can see,
without it's her last sickness; an' she's got a word
of courage for everybody. Life ain't spoilt her a
mite. She's eighty-six an' I'm sixty-seven, and I've
seen the time I felt a good sight the oldest.
'Land sakes alive!' says she, last time I was out
to see her. 'How you do lurch about steppin' into
a bo't!' I laughed so I liked to have gone right
over into the water; and we pushed off, an' left
her laughin' there on the shore."

Sarah Orne Jewett

LEGEND AND FICTION AND FACT superimpose one another in any accounting of the people of the coast.
They exist as stage types or stereotypes; they are
figures of comedy, or sentiment, or stern melodrama; their
voices are imitated on records and by countless amateur
tellers of funny stories. The Maine coast accent remains
the strongest and most distinctive of all the old regional
Yankee dialects. Perhaps the coast people have kept their
separateness better than any other group, though a sort of
cultural communism is overspreading all.

Once many decades ago I anchored for the night in a
harbor near Jonesport and a boy rowed out in a punt to
visit a bit and talk about the world. When he found out I
went to college he said he aimed to go too, and when I

asked him what college he looked at me with a kind of cautious suspicion. "Why," he said, "up to Orono. That's where the college is, ain't it?" In those days eastern Maine was a far country, off by itself. But I went on to ask him why he wanted to go to college, and his answer shot back quick. "Why, to git a girl!" A serious answer, tinged with contempt for a naïve question. He was a couple of years younger than I was, and may still be living east of Jonesport, with or without his girl. He knows now there is more than one college in the land; he is familiar with everything that goes on in the world, as transmitted to him by what sociologists call the mass media—perhaps he is more convinced than ever that the main purpose of college is to provide boy with girl and vice versa.

And his accent remains unchanged, and is passed on to the children and grandchildren, some of whom by now may be engineers in Alaska or geologists in Pakistan. It is deep-rooted and antique, that accent. It has Chaucerian and Shakesperian overtones. The word "boat" is pronounced as it is spelled, or perhaps as Chaucer would have said it; so also words such as "road" and "coat." Words with "edge" in them, like "wedge," "ledge," or "edge," are given a long, easy vowel sound, like "waydge" and "laydge." Short "a" is very flat in such words as "bar," which is spoken as "ba-a-," or "harbor," which sounds like "hab-ba." "Starboard" is "stabbud." The "r" is not sounded in "port" or "horn" or "corn." The "ing" ending is carefully and deliberately pronounced "in"—not slurred or mumbled, but almost accented. "Morning" becomes "maw-nin" with a pleasant emphasis on the "nin." I remember when I was a boy asleep in the little cabin of my sloop in Carver's Harbor I woke to unusual noises, and crawled out to see what was going on. It was two o'clock, a cloudless sky of stars and silver moon, and right above me loomed the bow of a trawler with a man standing in silhouette against the moon. They were just getting under way, and he was coiling a line. "Maw-nin, cap'n," he called down in the cheeriest voice I ever heard, "nice maw-nin, ain't it?" The words have sounded in my memory for forty years: I can still hear that explosive, joyous, ironic phrase. The very accent of it told me all about his life and my life.

It is presumed that the Maine speech is Yankee speech in general, and certainly there is a strong family resemblance, but to anyone who has heard it and used it for long the difference is striking. You hear a voice in some far place—New York or San Francisco or Panama—and you know at once it is a down-east voice: if you have nerve you can go up and say to it, "Is your name Eaton?" You'll be close enough to score a point. "Why, you must have in mind my cousin Nawm. Haskell's my name." Or Greenlaw, or Dow, or Pickering, or Pressey, or Brown, Black, Green, or Gray. In the two centuries they have lived on the coast they have made no changes in their speech or their names.

The accent is most pronounced in the children, where a strong intonation carries more meaning than the separate words. An outsider finds the speech of Maine children almost incomprehensible, specially when they are together and spontaneous. They speak with explosive enthusiasm, as though they had more vital energy than words to go with it; they seem to take pleasure in their special vocal sounds, and what comes out is the bits and pieces of a familiar recitative which is music to their own ears. Fragments of words shoot out like pellets, with all the force on one syllable and almost none on the rest, and what gives meaning is not so much the articulation of any one word as the rhythm or even the melody of a group of words. Unless you know what the native melodies are you may be quite lost in the flow of sound. It is partly a matter of a group of insiders recognizing themselves and enjoying their own separate security: this is the way *we* talk here; these are the passwords; *this* is the recognized accent, anyone who talks different is obviously an outsider. The adults carry on with it, but more gently and subtly. The childish explosions level off to a quieter rhythm, the articulation becomes more responsible, but the intonations are basically similar. Occasionally an adult carries on the habits of his childhood, and if he speaks to you at all does so as though he were firing his syllables at you through a mouthful of marbles.

Many an outsider who settles on the coast tries to adopt the speech as a way of being accepted and admired, and the result may be ludicrous; he finds himself talking like a stage Yankee from a nineteenth-century melodrama. A doctor of philosophy in one village has been eager to take part in its affairs, and speaks in town meeting with what he believes is the standard local dialect: he carefully drops his "g"s, puts in or leaves out his "r"s as the case seems to require, tries to say "road" exactly as it is spelled: but everyone addresses him and refers to him as "the professor" with an irony he has no defense against. It would of course be better for him to stick to whatever speech is native to him.

There are several key words that act as shibboleths, specially nautical ones. The unwary may say "gale" instead of "breeze," or "rib" instead of "timber." He misuses the word "rope," perhaps. (It has been said that the only ropes in a vessel were bolt ropes.) Or he may say "on" a vessel when he means "in." But the most frequent error is the lubberly misuse of the words "northeast" and "southeast": nothing gives an outsider, or a landsman, away quicker than those—specially "northeast." It is assumed by journalists and summer folk that the traditional contractions are "nor'east" and "sou'east," and such spellings are common in popular writings and publicity releases; but of course they are phoney, and betray the sort of ignorance that the user is making a special effort to be superior to. He is put in the position of the adult who talks down to children by heartily misusing their vocabulary. As I understand the tradition, the compass courses, the most vital lifelines of a ship, were passed from one steersman to another by speech: north, north and by east, north northeast—and always in the eastern quadrants the "th" was clearly and firmly pronounced. "Northeast" became "notheast" or "nothe-east," and "southeast" remained pretty much as it is spelled, with a soft "th" sound. In the western quadrants the "th" was dropped—hence "nor'west" and "sou-west." Chances of error or misunderstanding were lessened.

Language is what it is. If enough writers and speakers continue to misuse such a word as "demean," for example, it loses its original and accurate reference and in time the false meaning becomes the true one. The coast people still use "nothe-east" as opposed to "nor'west," and they still recognize the word "nor'east" or "nor'easter" as a sign of ignorance and pretense, but perhaps in time the old logic will disappear and the journalistic usage will prevail. It still seems preposterous to encounter cruisers in sail or power named *Nor'easter*, but the multiplying motels and restaurants and gift shops so named are the sort of flood we are borne along on. "Motel" was also once a word unacceptable and even incredible to purists. "Boatel" is perhaps worse. We are back in the old and never-ending argument as to the degeneration of our social order.

But reference to compass points used to be a common habit in all affairs, on or off salt water. Two men moving a kitchen stove muttered the course bearings to each other: edge her a mite nor'west, swing that end round to the suth'ard. I remember how George Dodge—pronounced always "Jawdge-dawdge"—gave his directions with a stammer. He said "nor-nor-nor'west" or "sou-sou-southeast," and if there was a gang working for him someone muttered that they'd be on the rocks sure with orders like that—only he muttered it softly because George Dodge had a famous temper. He once dropped a mooring under water, not far beyond low tide mark, with bearing from a point on shore, but whether it was "nor'west" or "nor'-nor'west" no one ever knew, and the mooring must be still there, forty years later. It shows how vital it is to transmit directions accurately. George had been to sea, of course, but I don't know how many orders he confused. One of his annual tasks in his later years was to set out a spindly pier on the shore near the cottage of a Boston family—and his orders to his gang were nautical and precise, except for the stammer, and profane—as suited his temper. I can still hear him as he spoke to one of the Boston ladies after the work was done. She had come down to see: she was elderly and timid—they were all elderly, and the pier was there only as a ritual commemorating an earlier time when they had had a boat. "It looks pretty rickety, Mr. Dodge. Do you think it will hold us all right?" "Oh, it'll *hold* you," he said with a flare of anger that the question had had to be asked. "It'll h-h-hold you, as long as you d-d-don't raise h-h-hell on it." And in memory of his temper let it be recorded that one day when a little grandson came and knocked on his door he yanked it open and spoke the words that are still quoted in his neighborhood: "God damn it, boy, your g-g-grandma has just f-f-fell down the cellar stairs and s-s-stove herself all to hell."

But though the old speech could be profane, and young boys learned to use the words boys use everywhere, what prevailed in general use was gentleness and kindliness. The tones of the old voices were melodic with concern for the enduring trials of living; some women almost crooned their compassion, and the sight of the very young and very old filled them with tender grief. Old men addressed their friends of both sexes as "dear" (pronounced "dee-ah" with rising emphasis on the last syllable), a habit so common that no one took note of it. Perhaps there is something in the life of a seaman that makes him compassionate and large of soul: certainly it makes him patient and full of concern for the safety and well being of others; he has learned responsibility, and practices it at home as well as abroad. Even the terrible-tempered George Dodge, as eloquent in cuss-words as an angry red squirrel, was as kindly and helpful among his neighbors as a man could be, and was both loved and respected.

If the tones and rhythms of speech reflect the quality of a people, these can be defined as both serene and vigorous. The gentle rhythms have a comforting effect, and the melody carries along from phrase to phrase, riding on the small connecting words like the repeated affirmative "ay-uh" or the intoned negative "no-o-o," with a sigh, perhaps, to invoke a patient acceptance of all human trials. But the old childlike energy is implicit too, the small explosions of sound, the tendency to give inflection to the last syllable of familiar names like Bangor, or Neville, or Haskell, or Bunker (Bunk-ah). I remember a telephone girl at Deer Isle trying to get through to Ellsworth, calling out a quiet and modulated "Deer Isle" and getting no response, then repeating it with emphasis, "Deer *Isle*," then at last shouting in the full force of her impatience, "Wul, Deer I-yull!" as though the final fortissimo would get through anything.

The speech is full of implicit courtesy, too. It may be nasal, like most American speech, but it nearly always carries a tone of kindness, perhaps even an awareness that part of the business of speech is to be beautiful, or at least touched with grace. And in this it may be contrasted with the graceless and ugly jargon that is spoken in the great cities—in Boston, for example, where what is now known throughout the land as a "Boston" accent seems mainly suited to barrooms and street corners and ward politicians.

The academic linguists of late years have adopted a behaviorism approach. Speech, they tell us, evolves and functions like the natural world. The question to ask about it is never what it should be, but what it is. There are no theoretical values, and a preference for Addisonian usage, say, merely reflects a delusion of elegance which has been promulgated by the Anglican establishment. To say that one word, or one accent, is better than another is like saying that a white heron is a better bird than a hawk, or a deer is better than a fox. Such judgments are prejudices and sentimental. In England a man could not succeed in public life without a gentleman's accent; in America very often he may not succeed with one. Hence any concept of correct speech and correct usage is merely a reflection of changing social prejudices. In language there is no "correctness." There is only function.

But language is also art, or the stuff of art. It may "function" as inevitably as the natural forces of demand and supply, but it not only expresses but embodies in itself esthetic values. It achieves beauty. It makes effective form. It invokes pleasure or sorrow. Its success is to be judged and measured. It may be good or bad, or anything between, and the student or user must be constantly observant of its values. In many ways it is like music—in some ways it is music, and the listener inevitably becomes a critic. He approves or disapproves by reference to a set of complicated and traditional values he is hardly aware of, a mixture of prejudice and logic and cultural habit. Lord Chesterfield defined good taste as the taste expressed by the "best people" in a society, and by the best people he meant the aristocracy of western Europe. Perhaps most of our traditional notions of good art and good manners have been shaped that way.

So the speech of the Maine coast represents a provincial

minority, and seems quaint and incorrect. A clinical linguist might accept it as an interesting fact, much as a
botanist would record and define a species of regional
tree, but the "best people" would find it unacceptable and
therefore wrong. Yet the linguist might note its respectable
ancient lineage, its accurate phonetic rendering of certain
words and its use of salt-water terms and a few old relics
long since forgotten by the rest of the world—"frock,"
for example, to mean a man's jacket, or the verb "bait,"
to mean feeding a horse or cow. The language spoken in
any long-settled region, like Scotland, say, is as "pure"
in a traditional sense as any language can be, and so it is
in Maine where the fashion of speech seems to reflect
usages learned centuries back in the old country. But of
course tradition in itself may be less than a virtue. American
speech in general has been developing as a sort of indigenous operation for nearly two centuries, and has built
up a strong tradition of its own, but it is still for the most
part "bad"—that is, it is nasal, throaty, fuzzily inarticulate,
and to most sensitive ears crude. The speech of eastern
cities, notably Boston and New York, is the worst, but
the hollow mouthings of the Middle West are almost as
flagrant. Perhaps Chesterfield's criterion of "best people"
is hard to find—and doubtless it no longer makes sense in
an unsegregated world. But an unbiased listener would
find a kind of beauty in Maine talk. It has a striking melody
and rhythm, sharp articulation, and an eager accent that
seems to take pleasure in the shape and ring of a word. And
at best it expresses consideration and human trust, not in
terms of sentiment or show, but simply as a mutual recog-
nition of decent intentions and truth.

FIVE

SUMMER FOLK

Watching the funeral gave one a sort of pain.
I began to wonder if I ought not to have walked
with the rest, instead of hurrying away at the
end of the services. Perhaps the Sunday gown I had
put on for the occasion was making this disastrous
change of feeling, but I had now made myself and
my friends remember that I did not really belong
to Dunnet Landing.

Sarah Orne Jewett

THEY HAVE ALWAYS BEEN second-class citizens in
Maine. No matter what the hopes and sentiments
are, they remain outsiders, they come "from away,"
they don't vote, attend town meeting, belong to the PTA,
and for the most part they have money and do no visible
work. They have been traditionally seen as incompetent
and soft, in need of care and protection against the natural
forces. They provide jobs and business, and pay taxes; they
are recognized as assets—more, as essentials to the economic welfare—and are treated accordingly. But the
relationship is at best much more than this: it can be
affectionate, mutually respectful, and by now traditional.
The patterns change with changing times, but a sort of
permanence has established itself over the greater part of
a century; there are "cottages," as all summer places are

persistently called, where four generations have come, and still come.

There are many kinds of summer folk, but these are the chief ones: the old families, the rich, the spinsters, the two-weekers (once the boardinghouse and hotel clients, now renters of cabins and camps), the retired (over sixty-five), and the passing tourists.

It was a paradise for old families, the quiet and proper Bostonians, the teachers and clergy, who practiced plain living and high thinking. They lived in the beautiful Emersonian world, with money enough to be comfortable but never ostentatious, with faith in the harmonies of nature and devotion to both beauty and duty. They read serious books by Darwin and Ruskin, big novels by Eliot and Mrs. Humphry Ward, and brought their children up on Lewis Carroll. They were probably all in all the best people the world has ever produced, a kind, cultivated, high-minded company, with good taste, good manners, humor, and genuine human sweetness. Their great fault was that they knew too little of the world's evil, and lived out their good lives in a delusion of faith and hope. They roused the resentment and jealousy of outsiders and others less fortunate who still denounce them for their innocence and their well-being. And doubtless complacence and even hypocrisy often find root in such soil.

But they were a real people: they were doctors, philosophers, professors, college presidents—many from Boston, but also from New York and Philadelphia and other academic areas. They came north and east for the summer not as transients but as serious settlers, and built the big shingled "cottages," with gables and porches, all unfinished and unpainted inside, smelling of fragrant new spruce—and done in those simple times with modest expense, with very low wages and plentiful cheap lumber. At first, in the decades after the Civil War, they boarded—sometimes in wooden boardinghouses built for the purpose, expanding into the larger and larger monstrosities of wood and shingles, and sometimes in the ordinary farm and village houses —as the author of *The Country of the Pointed Firs* boarded with Almira Todd at Dunnet Landing (a semimythical place that might be anywhere from Port Clyde to Stonington). The boarding arrangements were friendly and affectionate and semipermanent: people came year after year for long stays and looked on their visits as fundamental to their way of life. It was not only that the place itself was so cool and beautiful, but it offered the kind of human strength and warmth that Miss Jewett translated into the pages of her book. The pleasures were all simple and native, and the essential business of everybody had to do with fishing or farming. There was no society as such, no entertainment or planned games or golf or tennis— nothing but the boats, the shores and islands, the people and their traditions. From here it all seems Edenlike—and I think actually it was.

And even the vast hotels, like colossal matchboxes, shared in these simplicities. The same people came year after year with a strong feeling of proprietorship, and whole families consorted in a harmony of similar tastes and pleasure. In the best of this tradition there were no social directors or programs, no formalities of clothes or class, and people did what they felt like doing—restrained, doubtless, by the fundamental proprieties of an age of innocence. I remember a great barracks of a place on a point near Manset, on Mount Desert, called the Stanley House and run by the daughter of the Duck Island lighthouse keeper—a wholly native and local operation where the same families settled down for a couple of months and passed the time in sailing and fishing and climbing mountains and reading good books. They were academic people, many from Harvard, and elderly professors in white canvas hats rowed for exercise and pleasure, and in the evening one read aloud from Kipling. And of course they sat in rocking chairs on the long verandah and looked at the harbor and the boats and the panorama of islands and mountains. It was the fortunate world and time of William Dean Howells.

They were the ones who built the first cottages, and settled in quiet little regions far from the world's contaminations, and since many communities were built up on the basis of family and friends they achieved an innocent sort of exclusiveness: they lived simply and plainly, minding their own business, sailing modest little boats, rowing for exercise, exploring the remote islands, and developing in time a sort of Maine-coast style of life so that such a community as North Haven could become a complete little summer world of its own, a seasonal Shangri-La where age never withers and custom never stales, and the old ways go on unchanged among the same people for ever.

Or so it seems to an outsider. The children do the things their fathers used to do, and the fathers and grandfathers go on doing what they always did. Same clothes, same speech, same tastes. The wooden houses still smell with the same fresh woody smell, mixed with the faint sea damp of the old clothes, slickers, sneakers, kept from season to season, and bags of sails in closets, or the whiff of rope or tarred marlin, or even the skiff stored over the winter in the living room. And all the annual rituals of that life go on, the happy reunion with the plumber, the carpenter to fix the sagging porch, the man for the float and moorings—associates of a lifetime: and the anxious inspection of boats, the launchings and fitting out. . . .

The life goes on, at Northeast Harbor, Isle au Haut, North Haven, Islesboro, and many other small domains, but change and time are all-powerful. Those long idle summers seem far away and long ago. The old summer folk were not really a leisure class, nor parasites of any sort: they were professionals geared to a slower-paced world, and their students and scholars were not driven by the relentless competition of today. Summer schools hardly existed. A scholar was permitted to reflect critically and philosophically. A clergyman could close his church for a couple of months, and a college dean or president assumed that the place would pretty much take care of itself in the hot weather. And with time the domestic economy has changed: those shingled houses required "help," and help is no longer possible. In one of her essays Virginia Woolf refers to "one's cook," as though all respectable people of her world naturally had a cook, but there are few cooks in the modern economy. Nor are there "men" to tend to boats and moorings and all heavy work. Many of the rituals of the old life have to be abandoned, and many of the houses themselves are too inconvenient and inaccessible. Some stand empty, and some are demolished.

The rich, so far as I know, exist still, but their habits are also different. Perhaps there are only a few basic ways of spending money, and houses and yachts are still prominent, but the old time of conspicuous display is gone. A yacht such as J. P. Morgan's *Corsair* seems now as remote and incredible as the visions of ancient Persepolis, yet I used to see her looming hugely against the Maine landscape. The great fire put a period to the Bar Harbor era, but it was over and done with anyway. Doubtless they may still be seen there, the rich, or at Seal or Northeast, or even at Islesboro, but they seem to be a somewhat different breed. The people who made Bar Harbor into a resort had no interest in Maine life or tradition, and were simply buying a beautiful site and climate for their own worldly pleasures. They succeeded in destroying the indigenous quality of that part of Mount Desert, which is now the least characteristic place on the coast. In the celebrated exchange between Fitzgerald and Hemingway on the subject of the rich it strikes me that Fitzgerald had a point that the more arrogant Hemingway missed. The rich *are* different from the rest of us, not only because they have more money, but because they can ignore so many of the values that seem essential to us. Anyone who can build a house on the coast of Maine and install gold bathroom fixtures is not in any normal sense quite human —and such blindness used to be characteristic of the capitalistic royalty who purchased whatever pleased them.

Perhaps it no longer is. The word now is affluence, and so many have it that the older symbols of ostentation seem absurd and even vulgar. The big yachts are now seventy feet instead of three hundred and the palaces no longer stand out like Hampton Court but merge into the landscape with an effect of seclusion and secrecy. And since the world has grown restless and the rich are less idle than they used to be and the summers are shorter, the elaborate establishments have dwindled. Last year the great gabled château of the Rockefellers at Seal Harbor was torn down, with all its music rooms, drawing rooms, squash courts, butler's pantries, servants quarters, and offices, and now the gardens and grounds are park for the pleasure of all.

But I don't really know much about the rich, past or present. They were and are part of the Maine scenery. They used to be alien and seemed quite preposterously artificial: but as a long-range view, Hemingway's may be right after all. They are simply people with more money. In the equalitarian future we are coming to, the rich will presumably no longer exist as a class. Nor the poor.

The spinsters, though, will be with us always—and I include all semi-independent ladies with small inheritances who can afford a cottage in the true sense, a modest little dwelling, a native village house, a "camp" by the shore, and a half acre of land. Many are schoolteachers, relishing every free minute of their ten-weeks summer, dreaming of the day when they can live in their little Edens from May to October. Maine is full of them. They take pride in merging with the native life; they assist at the fairs and food sales, join rug-hooking groups, go to lectures, to exhibitions, to church, join in on picnics and excursions. They are devoted to plain living and plain thinking. They have little to do with the old salt-water life of the coast, but they are expert in the domestic traditions and are connoisseurs of antiquities. They pick up old milking stools and washstands at auctions, or embroidered framed samplers, or pickle crocks, or oil lamps; they make dandelion wine not because they like wine but because the recipe is irresistible; they make a jar or two of wild cranberry sauce to take back with them for Thanksgiving and Christmas. They are for the most part quite inconspicuous, and blend into the life of the region, but they are everywhere, and sometimes—at an evening lecture with color slides of the Greek islands—you see them in great number. They help the regional economy, but more than that they supply a kind of honest, warm-hearted human substance that enriches the community life. A casual observer would hardly realize that such a group existed at all.

The two-week vacationers come from everywhere, with stationwagons full of family, rent whatever is available, and next year perhaps go elsewhere. Some bring all their boats and equipment with them; others scurry around to find amusements and sights to see. They complain of their hard lot in having only two weeks, and hope for a more liberal future. They tend to patronize the more popular centers like Boothbay Harbor and Mount Desert, and many come equipped to camp out at the organized public camp grounds. They are often happy, sometimes carefree, and devote themselves enthusiastically to vacation pleasures: some even take eagerly to nature and go on walks to look at the woods and shores with a group and a guide. But most of them are careless strangers, with no share in the region itself. The state of Maine has persuaded itself to print the word "Vacationland" on its automobile license plates, which implies that the state exists chiefly as a recreational business; but in a sense it is selling its own birthright. The main-traveled roads are already turning into extended midways.

But of course the strangers will keep coming, and their money is essential to a region that has too little to live on anyway. The balance is precarious. Through all of time the world has been blighted and laid waste by the money-makers—or simply by people in the careless act of living. Jonathan Swift called them vermin—meaning all of us.

The coast itself, the very edge of the land, is a harsh place in winter. Unchecked wind whistles through the cracks of the tightest house, damp seeps in, metals rust, on coldest days sea smoke blows in and covers windows and walls with salt rime. The old-timers built well away from the shore. On sea-girt Matinicus the settlement is mostly in the middle of the island. So old-timers today, looking for what the real-estate people advertise as "retirement homes," are wary of too much saltwater exposure, and tend to prefer the landbound villages where the winter sun is more benign and the wind loses its force among trees and hills.

Many of them are erstwhile summer folk who make the grave decision to abandon their city or suburban world and settle for life in the land they have spent their vacations in. And it may be that many have hopes of merging with their new communities as citizens and even natives, but I think the true experience of most is that though they are often welcomed as friends and neighbors they are in fact kept forever in a separate category as outsiders. By blood and habit New Englanders are stern traditionalists, specially the outlying inhabitants of the north and east where the world's contamination is less, and out of this traditionalism—so conscious of ancestral ways and memories—comes an impervious complacence. *We* do it this way, we don't need any advice from outsiders. . . .

There are times of crisis when newcomers of a year, or perhaps of five years or even ten, are stunned by the latent hostility of a normally friendly community. They have settled with good intentions and kindly expectations, they have made friends, gone to socials, served at church fairs, and suddenly in the heat of an angry town meeting are denounced and damned as alien trouble makers.

The essential problem, of course, is the necessity of raising and spending tax money, and nothing is more painful to any Yankee community. The very idea of taxes makes them angry. They assume that all outsiders and city people are full of extravagant visions of new schools, libraries, parks, and other public expenditures, and they realize that a large slice of their tax money comes from these same outsiders: what results is a feeling compounded of guilt, jealousy, parsimony, and old-fashioned pride. Emotions explode, bitter words are spoken, feelings are hurt, a sense of bewilderment and frustration emerges. The political habits of the New England town have been praised over the years as reflecting an ideal democratic process, but to any participant, whether insider or outsider, they seem at times to bring out the most unlovely traits in human nature.

So the settlers from away learn perforce to be humble and to pay their taxes quietly, with no implied advice as to how the money should be spent. If they go to town meeting they find it safer to sit in the rear and say nothing.

In time, in ten or twenty years, they may with all due modesty contribute an idea or a talent or skill, and the man who was once a university president, say, may even in due course be asked to fill in as moderator—if he lives that long.

But unless miracles occur, the world of the summer folk will prevail. They bring the money. And tourists pour in like an irresistible force. The road from Ellsworth to Bar Harbor in July and August is like the narrow spout of a funnel whose wide intake is the nation itself. To the passing motorist the coast is chiefly a spectacle of motels, drive-ins, gift shops, antique shops, restaurants, and signs. He gets a few glimpses of blue water, of shoreside eating places offering lobster in all possible form, and he achieves finally the climactic summit of Cadillac Mountain, which is beautiful (when free of fog), and the outer drive round Otter Cliffs, which is even more beautiful, fog or no fog. Those are the scenes they drive across half the continent to see. They know that Maine itself exists—they have read of it and heard of it, and they drive in a sort of illusion that somewhere it must actually have its being; but they seldom get close to it, and if its reality in truth grows less and less they are the ones, as emissaries of the nation of the future, who are most effectively destroying it.

SIX

BOATS

> Of all fabricks a ship is the most excellent,
> requiring more art in building, rigging, sayling,
> trimming, defending, and moaring, with such a
> number of several termes and names in continual
> motion, not understood of any landsman, as none
> would thinke of, but some few that knew them.
>
> *Captain John Smith*

MEN LOOK AT GREAT SHIPS AND LITTLE SHIPS with the same sort of appraisal. The sheer of a liner can seem spiritual—or beautiful in some unexplained way; so also can a dory be beautiful. Whether ten feet or a thousand, a ship is a ship. The great schooners and the smallest sloops used to be timbered, caulked, rigged, equipped, and even handled exactly the same. When you see a yacht under sail at a little distance with no scale, nothing to measure her by, you can't tell if she's an ocean cruiser or a day sailer manned by ten-year-olds. Nothing made by man comes closer to animation. Every ship acquires what we call character. We like her, dislike her—we can love her, hate her, we are moved with admiration or disgust. Men marry ships as legally as they marry women, and suffer the same trials, feel the same kind of fidelity and responsibility, have the same pride and

You saw the big ones offshore, beating westward, all topsails set

patience, and the same dream of a beauty and perfection just beyond mortal reach.

Since the first logs and bundles of reeds were manned the form of the hull has evolved and responded to need and function. It should by now be final. But I think every designer of a skiff or a cup defender begins with a vision of such elegance and performance as the world has never yet seen. Perfection is always ahead, beckoning. Hull form may have attained a classic finality here and there— in a Viking long ship, say, or a Baltimore clipper, or a Maine peapod—but he hardly admits it, and he knows that new materials lead to new perfections. If he is working with power and great speed he is in the midst of innovation.

But Maine ships were the wooden ones, and achieved ideal form from the little double-enders called peapods, like small domesticated whale boats, to the great full-rigged downeasters, the last and most splendid of the age of sail. The big schooners were native to Maine: I remember them lying in every port waiting with infinite patience for wind and tide, five-masters, six-masters, with their long, long sheer line sweeping forward to the great bowsprit and jib boom with all the heavy rigging of chains, stays, martingale, knightheads. In the fresh north-westers they kited off, out of the bays and harbors, running free on the starboard tack, topsails, staysails, flying jibs all set and molded to the wind, twelve knots—maybe fifteen, steady and grand in the bright sunlight. At all times of day you saw schooners in the offing, two masters working through the channels and reaches, bucking tides, tacking among ledges, sluggish and slow, cargoes of stone, lumber, bales of hay; or you saw the big ones offshore, beating westward, long and short hitches, hull down over the edge, all topsails set and showing against the white of the horizon sky. Hard-working ships, weathered, moldy, coal-blackened, patched, fighting a losing battle in a changing world, but part of the old age of the sea and backed by a host of trained workers, builders, smiths, riggers, caulkers, sailmakers, and seamen. A whole world and life, all gone.

Every deep cove on the coast once had its resident sloop lying at mooring or grounded beside a wharf. If you came as a stranger, groping in through foggy or dusky channels, you expected her; you at once looked for her as the local guardian or divinity, and even in gathering darkness you saw the distinctive profile that has remained one of the classic strokes of boat design. How many times in my youth has the white form taken shape against a dusky shore, the low freeboard aft sweeping upward in a noble curve toward the clipper bow and then subtly reversing itself and running out to the long bowsprit—a line of beauty, as old Hogarth would have called it, so delicate that sketchers and painters never quite get it: the Maine sloop, the Friendship sloop (not always built in Friendship), came as near sharing man's spirit as anything ever built of oak and pine and galvanized nails. She gave a new character to the loneliest waters. She was always a reassurance, a message that a good man had conceived and made her, a triumph of function and elegance in a world of rock and fog and storm. She is still vivid in my old dreams, her silhouette in a remote cove, the white-topped mast way forward, stayed forward, the long white boom cocked over the stern, moving a little on its topping lift, the gray

Hard-working ships, weathered, moldy, coal-blackened, patched,
fighting a losing battle in a changing world

canvas loosely gathered, and the beautiful sweep of the sheer, mounting and mysteriously curving. She was the emblem of the old coast life.

With all that look of grace she could be a brutal boat. Heavy gear, long spar, long sprit, harsh weather helm, slow to windward—but always reliable—or nearly always: I remember a day of gusty northwest wind when the *Linnie Belle* swamped and sank and drowned many people —and no doubt she was over-sailed and badly handled. They used to say a Friendship sloop could "go anywhere," and some have, and now they preserve and build them as yachts, and there is a kind of fervor about the process that makes me think once more of that old touch of divinity the sloops once had as though somehow they carried some spiritual mystery within their timbers.

It is romantic to say it this way, but without romance we are better dead. I lived as a child in a dream of boats, I drew them, whittled them, sailed them in tide pools, watched them near and far, listened to talk about them. I hoarded pictures. I knew the names and the look of the great yachts: the *Reliance*, fastest of all Cup defenders, the *Defender* herself, "with her crew of Deer Islers," as the caption said—a detail I've never forgotten because in a small way I was a Deer Isler too. And the splendid schooners, *Enchantress*, *Irolita*, *Elena*, *Queen Mab*, and the *Atlantic*, three-masted, breaking all records for an eastward crossing to England—the picture of her charging to windward under full sail, all topsails set, is still as dramatic as anything I can remember. They had nothing to do with earthly life, those boats; they were pure visions, and reflected a romance not of mortal people and their concerns but rather of triumphant speed and grace and mastery of wind and sea. Herreshoff the designer was like a god and in the ancient Olympian hierarchy would have sat at the right hand of Poseidon; even now he seems more myth than man.

They were long-ended and low, with deep lead keels and huge spreads of sail. They were more beautiful, more mysteriously graceful, and probably faster than anything under sail today, but they represented a more fantastic extravagance—it is hard to believe that the old *Reliance*, for example, could have been anything but a dream. But all yachts are dreams, and I grew up among them—I grew old among them. I filled countless margins and notebooks with sketches, mostly abortive. The lovely long sheer and overhangs of a William Gardner sloop, like the *Vanitie*, say—could I ever quite get it on paper? Or the subtle reversing curves of a Friendship? Or a Banks dory? If you want to put a sketcher to the test, set him to draw a dory. There's something in such craft beyond the lines themselves; there's an animation as though the thing had breath and soul. My everlasting sketching never quite succeeded: the beauty and truth I sought always eluded—just barely eluded me by the smallest of margins.

I took to serious designing, with drawing boards and instruments. I even came close to trying to make a career of it, and once wrote to one of the great ones of boat designing, Starling Burgess, to ask advice, and I remember his courteous reply and invitation to come and talk with him. I was a very young man then, younger than I should have been at twenty-three, and I was in love, my vision of boats was like love, but I drew back from it—some

A line of beauty, as old Hogarth would have called it

ancestral puritan voice warned me that yachts were too lovely, too pleasant and delightful, to spend a life with. I must turn to a sterner sort of reality, I thought. It may be that I wanted to keep them as a dream, that I had too little faith in my illusions. I never went to see Starling Burgess, who later designed the great Cup defender *Ranger*, undefeated and unrivaled among class-J boats.

But I went on designing. I read books in an amateurish sort of way; I spent evening hours poring over lines and sections and buttocks, and I figured and refigured displacements with confusing and inaccurate results. Science has taken more and more charge of it, but forty years ago boat building, specially in Maine, was a sort of folk art. A man could whittle out a half model, shape it by eye, and expect it to prosper. Experience was the essential. And in fact the powerboats now used by Maine fishermen, a distinctive and successful and quite beautiful type, have been achieved by the same old evolutionary method and are still being refined by local whittlers and builders—the last stand, perhaps, of the wooden boatbuilding tradition. I plunged into it, anyway—getting my small experience by haunting boat yards and brooding over designs and sailing whatever boats came my way. In time a few friends and relatives took a kindly interest and a boat of my design was actually contracted for. A quite splendid boat, as it turned out, a sloop thirty-five feet long with cabin room for at least four and full cruising equipment.

At that time, forty years ago, having a boat built in Maine involved both social and temperamental problems. You knew that Roy Coombs was recognized as an able boatbuilder, and when you went to open negotiations his

wife said he was off taking a bargeload of sheep to Hard-
wood Island. Next time he'd gone over to Pleasant River
to help dynamite some stumps. Next time you found him
on a scaffold painting the Methodist Church. He could
build a boat for you—his face lit up with pleasure and
pride at the idea of a boat: he'd like for you to see the sloop
he built last year for some folks from Islesboro—he had
the half model down in the shop. . . . Right now, of course,
he had his hay to get in, and he'd promised to build the
fireplace and chimney for the new cottage on Cedar Island;
they kind of counted on using it this summer. And he was
working on a patent—"A what?" you said. A kind of automatic jack for cars—he'd like to show you, he had it down
at the shop. . . .

Next day at the shop you found him installing a new
engine in a lobster boat, a thirty footer that filled the
building and projected a few feet out the rear end. But
the sloop you had in mind was even bigger. . . . No trouble
about that, he said; he could knock out both end walls, he
could take out the floor and lower her down as much as
three feet. Suppose he drew out some plans—he had an
idea for a nice little boat for cruising; he'd make a model
first; he liked to build right off a model. As to an estimate,
a price, he'd have to figure it, of course, but he could generally come pretty close. He had the nicest cedar planking
you ever saw right there in the loft, and he knew where he
could get his hands on some good white oak—yes, he could
figure it close enough. Price, he implied, was the simplest
of his problems. He took up a slab of sun-dried codfish
from the workbench and passed it around. "Just take a
taste of that," he said with a glint of fanatical delight. "It's

some I brought in last spring, and I believe it's the best I ever tasted."

My part in this was that of a presumed yachting expert and consultant, and when the drawings came—on sheets of wrapping paper—I pronounced them wholly inadequate. I knew very little about the realities, of course; my head was full of visions of beauty and speed—and here on the wrapping paper was a stout and solid native model, close to the Friendship mold. I criticized it with youthful vehemence and prejudice, and was challenged to produce something better.

This is all in the main a true story. Roy Coombs was actually the man who built *Charmian*, and I have always taken credit for the design. I drew plans; I sent them to Roy—by this time summer was over; he made a half model and sent it back to me, and I was overwhelmed with delight and love. I have it now, the model, and can look at it with the same emotions. It was he who gave her her true spirit, and when the people of Vinal Haven used to call her Roy Coombs' boat they were right. But I am still known as her designer, and I am happy to take the credit. She has behaved beautifully for forty years. She is handsome, comfortable, and fast in all weathers. I gave her too much sail, of course, but with her big sail on she can beat anything in sight—at least that is one of the articles of faith that goes with my dream. The first summer of her life I remember coming out of Castine just behind the *Raider*, a racing sloop famous in the region, a long, fin-keeled, big-sailed beauty. Fresh southwest wind, say twenty knots, heavy tidal chop as there always is off Castine, both boats on the port tack, close-hauled—and *Charmian* outpointed and out-footed her rival. A true story.

But the building—two years of delay, hope, innocent confusion, and final triumph. Roy Coombs was a professional boatbuilder, no doubt about it. He did the work beautifully. He was also a professional mason, mechanic, modelmaker, inventor, photographer, and artist—I think his church murals are still to be seen in his town. He was a man full of visions, a small, wiry, eager, resourceful genius who began more things than he finished. His eyes shone with anticipations of his own ingenuity: andirons forged from kedge anchors, a dining table made from a ship's mahogany wheel, a popplestone fireplace, a steamer's pilothouse transformed to a shore cottage. On his ship models the windlass worked and the steering gear worked though the rest of them were never quite finished. He agreed to build *Charmian* over the winter, and in June when I arrived at his shop full of hope there was a two-ton iron keel and a curving stem timber like the neck of a dinosaur, and nothing else. They sat in the grass, outside the shop doors, with a somewhat weathered look. That was our boat.

Roy wasn't there at the time. He was two miles away, building a shore cottage.

But a two-ton keel was something. The rest, he implied, would take him no time at all—which in the end turned out to be a year. The keel had been cast and shipped from Camden, and he admired it very much. The oak deadwood and keel were the best oak, and he admired the precision of his work in setting them up. When he "timbered her out" with steam-bent double-curving timbers, and removed the molds and battens, he stood back and looked at his creation with glowing eyes. "Prettiest set of timbers you'll ever see," he said. By then it was August, and time no longer seemed to matter. The great thing was creation itself. The boat now filled his shop like Alice in the upper chamber, and projected into a shed he had built out over her stern. She was hard to see. But she was clearly there, body and soul emerging. When the planking went on she was full-grown. I watched; I participated, I measured and marked, and I was treated like a colleague. It was the best time of my youth. I remember climbing into the bare hull with Roy Coombs, among the chips of pungent new oak and fragrant new cedar, and measuring the available space with six-foot rules—marking cockpit area, cabin trunk, deck, hatches, with tentative berths, galley, head, lockers. He never sailed her—except once round the harbor: he had his own visions, through—the compact and ingenious workmanship, the special cypress for the cabin woodwork, the construction of the trunk, the clear pine strips for the deck, "Oh, you'll have some good cruising in her," he used to say—always pronouncing it with a sharp "s," as in "goose." He even said we'd have "good cruising" this summer, and seemed to believe it: he saw his work as finished long before the reality. It was another year before the cruising came to pass.

But nothing is more hopeful than a new ship. Old ones are tired; they grow limber; they work; fastenings give; timber weakens—there is no rest for any ship at sea. But a new one seems to have the strength of ten; it is the athlete in his prime. The metal is perfect; the timbers ring with life; she is all tight; she takes to winds and waves joyfully. And nothing is sadder than a new ship lost, even before she tests herself and fulfills the hopes and labors that went into her building. I suppose *Charmian* is old now—forty years, in fact; she has gone off to other waters. She probably leaks—her garboards doubtless work in a head wind and sea. But as long as she floats she will be herself, the individual with the mysterious boat-soul that has won the love of many people.

A small sequence of lucky accidents, and you get to be an expert—at least among family and friends. Five boats, each different, were built from my designs, and they are all still afloat; but as time goes on such enterprises are less and less possible. Anyone looking for a *Charmian* now would pick one of six or eight competing standardized models, turned out on production lines like Chryslers or Buicks, with fiberglass hulls and aluminum spars and up-to-the-minute equipment, and probably only a sentimentalist would want to revert to the folkways of building. It may be that oak and cedar are already anachronistic. Some day we will be looking back at the classic wooden hull with the sort of incredulous wonderment and respect we give to the other handmade miracles of the primitive eras, the stonework of cathedrals, for example. How could all those bits of stone, or wood, be shaped, fitted, fastened, and transformed into a vast new fabric?

The five boats exist, and each has a pretty decent character and reputation (I have to speak of them as a man would speak of his children), but I often wish I could mold and shape them a little. I note that expensive boats, like the contenders for Cup defense, can be reshaped, but the ordinary boat is fixed for life—in her fundamental body, at least. Rigs can change. *Charmian* did better with bow-

sprit and larger jib. Finding the exact balance was for me
a matter of guesswork, and so it is for those who are
supposed to know. Some hulls are so cussed they never
balance. Others are so docile they seem to sail themselves,
no matter what the rig—and such a one is *Festina*, the sloop
I designed for myself.

Not a masterpiece, I am sorry to say—at least after
twenty-five years I am aware of what she can and can't
do. She can't carry sail. In a wind over twenty knots she
needs reefing. But up to eighteen, say, she is the sweetest,
most lovable boat I ever knew. She goes to windward so
fast and close, with such a sense of joy, that she brings
tears to your eyes. No spray. No fuss, no wake—just a
lovely sort of eagerness as though nudging up into the eye
of the wind is what she was born to do. And reefed down
in a hard breeze she is the same way—she can slip through
a tidal chop as though it weren't there, and for some reason
unknown to her designer her decks stay dry. She is rather
low of freeboard; her cabin by current standards is small,
without headroom, and she is not pretty: I look at her with
the inward bewilderment of a man who wonders how he
ever got himself into his particular matrimonial trap, but
once she is off and moving, sheets tight in, rail down, tiller
gentle to the hand as she eats out to windward, she is
wholly beguiling. I realize that in this life, at least, I'll
never have a better boat.

She can run too, no faster perhaps than other fast boats
—not quite so fast as *Charmian*, who is larger, but she
runs with perfect ease and quietness. If it blows hard you
can furl the jib and she still steers as sweetly as ever. If it
blows too hard you can sail her under jib alone, and work

her to windward or any other way.

There was a time when the two boats used to cruise together, with daylong tooth-and-nail rivalry. The variables are infinite, also the luck. First one and then the other won out. Each had its own ideal conditions, and each could sail the other hull down in a day's run. Often enough I've seen that dead-white old gaff sail (the big one) of *Charmian's* slanting on the horizon ahead, and perhaps more often behind; but mostly I see it a hundred yards off the lee bow and I try to figure if she'll cross ahead or behind when she tacks.

The methods of *Festina's* building were the same: the oak and cedar, the molds and battens, the steam box, the nailed fastenings, but I specified bronze nails instead of galvanized iron, and regretted it. They didn't hold. Bronze doesn't bind with wood. So I had her screwed together with bronze screws, and she is still solid. The building was done in a yard on Deer Isle, in the late thirties, at a basic cost of about a sixth of what it would be now; she is rugged, plain, unvarnished—the only concession to modern materials was in the plywood decks, which at that time seemed to the builders a risky innovation—and even now a plain painted plywood deck is not quite acceptable in a yacht. But it works well. The rig, mast, stays, fittings, and sails (sails by Ratsey) were left over from an abandoned class-R boat—they were stored in a barn and would still be there if I hadn't liberated them for a price too small to mention. All too heavy, even when cut down, but I've used them ever since—even the Ratsey sail is usable, though tender (it tore across in a gale in Muscongus Bay). Of late I've had Dacron sails, like all other sailing men, and they

The purest ideal (in the Platonic sense) of the boat

arc beautiful; I even sometimes hope my old heavy mast will carry away at last and compel me to install lightweight aluminum—and then how elegantly would *Festina* go, how fast to windward, faster than anything ever seen in those parts.

But to be candid, the difference is only between six knots, say, and six and a half. That means speed in a sailing craft. It is all a state of mind. I read of catamarans that make twenty knots and hope they won't come to destroy my illusions.

When I was small I learned to row mostly in a ten-foot boat we called the tender, which is a name given to any small craft whose function it is to be an attendant on a larger craft, and generally to be towed. Our tender was simply a little rowboat, built at Crabtree Point in North Haven Island about the year 1903. It is now in its seventh decade. I can see it as I write, floating at an outhaul off my landing. Of all boats of any size I have seen, used, been in and out of over a sixty year span, this little one represents to me the purest ideal (in the Platonic sense) of the boat. She is not only perfect in function but she is quite subtly and mysteriously beautiful—yet what I call beauty in her belongs to her function. The marked sheer, for example: her freeboard all along is always exactly right for whatever she has to do. The little hollow of her water line forward, the flare of her bows, the curve of her stem, are as graceful as anything carved, but she will ride over all the rips and chops on the coast without shipping a cupful. Her run aft is almost the best part of her: she has a sturdy and steady look to her; she has good beam and bilges, yet her run is as fine as a racing shell's—or almost. She rows without

effort—I have rowed hundreds of miles in her over a lifetime. As such craft go she is not light; she has been
wrecked, rebuilt, reenforced, painted with many coats—
and her old pine planks are getting soft. She is only ten
feet long; in some ways she is out of date since she is not
meant for outboard power; but if there is any Platonic
heaven where the idea of Boat exists in divine perfection it
will be recognized as the original model for the little
tender.

Boats like most things are compromises. The comfortable ones may be slow, and the fast ones may drench or
drown their crew. Some are so comfortable they won't
move at all and function as floating houses. Some are deep
and powerful, like the old North Sea pilot vessels; others
like the Chesapeake skipjacks are shoal enough to float in
heavy dew. When you take on a boat for better or worse
you involve yourself in more variables and considerations
than you can ever be quite reconciled to. You find yourself casting a longing eye on the other man's boat—you
have glimpses of such beauty and charm as you had never
known before. You imagine miracles of performance. Life
with her, you think, would be a dream come true at last.

But in maritime history everything has been tried—or
almost everything. We leave room for miracles, chiefly in
the form of new materials and new power. Over the
centuries all shapes and sizes have appeared, some as
bizarre as the styles in ladies' clothes, some grimly func-
tional, some purely beautiful. The Viking long ships are
the emblems of speed and deadly purpose and pride. The
old trading caravels represented a stodgy feudal traditionalism where time had no value and ships were built to

resemble floating castles. Then eventually speed again, the Yankee brigs and topsail schooners of 1812, the privateers, oversparred and oversailed, symbols of youth and adventure, the fastest ships yet created—until the day of the great clippers just before the Civil War, those colossal and impossible racing machines that captured the world's fancy.

One of the technical words applied to the clipper ships is the adjective "extreme": the vessel *Lightning*, for one, is designated as an extreme clipper. Naval design tends toward the limits of possibility, and sometimes beyond. Deep and narrow hulls go to windward best—hence the ultimate "plank on edge" developed in Britain at the turn of the century. But flat and beamy hulls can carry more sail and run faster—hence the centerboard skimming dishes and sandbaggers popular in America at the same time. Freaks, we say, looking at their models in the marine museums. We see the necessity of compromise, of using common sense and achieving balance and all-round usefulness and good health. The yacht-racing gentry devise rules and formulae as preventives against extremism, with good practical results: the modern ocean racer, like the yawl *Ondine*, for one, is as fine a combination of speed and sea-going ability and power as the ordinary sailor can imagine. Yet the romantic dream always beguiles a few eternally hopeful designers and adventurers, the dream of ultimate performance and beauty. It is a commonplace of whimsy to observe that ships are feminine, but the fact is that men—Anglo-Saxon men, at least—have always looked upon them with sexual longing. Grim old Beowulf called his ship "the foamy-necked floater." Donald McKay, artist and dreamer and builder of the world's most beautiful wooden ships, named his last and best creation the *Glory of the Seas.*

SEVEN

WIND AND WEATHER

A calme, a brese, a fresh gaile, a pleasant
gayle, a stiffe gayle. It overblowes. A gust, a storme,
a spoute, a loume gaile, an eddy wind, a flake of
wind, a Turnado, a Mounthsoune, a Herycano.

Captain John Smith

IT IS WHAT PEOPLE DOWN THERE TALK ABOUT most of the
time. There is a great deal of it, for one thing—not so
much in storm and stress as in change. All New Englanders boast of weather, remembering what Mark Twain
said about it, but in Maine the pride and pleasure are even
greater. It pleases them that the broadcast reports are so
often wrong. If he'd just look out the window, they say,
instead of reading from his script, he'd know more about it.
As much as half the time, they say, he tells us it will be fair
to partly cloudy, with a chance of showers: that covers a
good many possibilities. As for the storm warnings, the
"small craft warnings" are so frequent it's like the boy
calling "wolf, wolf." All the official weather people, they
think, are way off in Boston or Washington anyway—
they don't really know what happens in Maine.

What happens is not necessarily violent, but there are

distinctive characteristics. It's the cold water, they say. That makes fog, anyway, and there's more fog in Maine than anywhere else except perhaps Nova Scotia—it gives them pleasure to say that too.

All along the coast there is what everyone thinks of as a "normal" day, and when it doesn't occur for long periods there are complaints. It may begin very early, at the first streak of morning with a northwesterly air, quite cold and piercing, like a breath of mountain country. Sun comes up clear in a very pale-blue sky—not much glow of sunrise color. There is a soaking dew, specially along the shores and harbors: your decks are a half-inch thick with it, and it flashes and sparkles in the new sunlight. The early northerly sets up a dark ripple on the waters; you hear the stretch of your anchor rope as the boat swings to it: but as the sun climbs and pours warmth into the cold air the breeze fades and vanishes, and the water reflects great flashes like molten enamel. All is perfectly still. If you have been asleep below you have felt the chill of that early land breeze with its mountainy air, but now the sun on deck transmits a new warmth and you lie basking, dreaming, hearing gull-talk and the quick notes of terns—not another sound or stir. Reflected sunlight flickers on the cabin roof above you. You know there's no breeze at all. You take it slow, wait for some spirit to move in you; the warmth and stillness are like a comfortable element you are suspended in.

If you have power, you can up anchor and be on your way, with noise and vibration. Otherwise you wait. Perhaps at ten o'clock an air stirs; and you see a little ruffled blue off the lee of a low shore. Do you risk it? You may as well drift as lie anchored, and perhaps you have run of tide in your favor. But you know the early breeze will be fickle; the little ruffles will always be somewhere else, and you will be fixed by the heat and glare—and if you manage to get out of the harbor into the wide waters you'll roll and slat. But you know too that the good breeze will come, you have no uncertainty: eleven, twelve—surely by then. You can feel the nature of the day. That cold dawn, the early northerly, the stillness, the very look of the air—you know each phase. On some days the good breeze comes late—one o'clock, or even two, or not at all; you think you can tell, though perhaps you don't know what the signs are. You simply feel it. But today is pure and classic—perhaps it is late August, when such days come best. Calm air is hot; sun is hot; but there is a vibration of life in it. And then, outside, where you can look off to the southern horizon, you see it, the straight edge of dark blue on the sea. Here all is still silvery in the calm, and your boat stirs idly and the limp sails flap a little—but there it comes, the breeze, the southwest wind, the main event of the coastal day. The line of it advances, you can see the quick sparks of sunlight and the pointed little dark-blue waves; it is like a rush of new life on the sea—perhaps you can hear it rustling as it comes, and you wait for it with wonderful expectation. Already the whole expanse of southern waters, out among far ledges and islands, is alive with the new wind.

And then you have it, you are in it, and your vessel springs into vibrant life. Everything tightens, stretches, sails, sheets, rigging; she pays off, leans, moves—starboard tack, offshore, out into it; water under the lee bow surging, rolling into foam, streaming along the lee, bubbling in the wake; your towing tender dances along behind, tiller nudges against your hand; you brace a foot against the lee seat; you look ahead for sea marks, and your mind's eye is full of courses made good and distances and far ports of call.

Now the day itself is upon you, the fine old Maine-coast day that everyone keeps in mind as the criterion of all good days. The wind is cold; you put on sweater and jacket—you forget that heat and calm of the morning; you feel the freshness in your lungs and chest—not the dry cold of the land, but softer, moister cold of northern sea. As the day settles down to its business you feel more and more alone out there. The breeze works itself gradually up from eight knots to twelve to fifteen and even to twenty, a cold, steady, determined pressure. Groundswell and wind come in at different angles, and with an ebbing tide running west and southwest a sort of cross rip develops, an irregular chop and surge, but easy and pleasant enough for an able boat—and if you stand offshore three or four miles on the starboard tack you find easier water and can fetch westward parallel to the coast on a long port tack.

In the afternoon a white haze comes in on the wind. The early morning clearness has long since gone, and now all things are dim and far. It is not fog, the day is still fine, the sun still pours into your cockpit and warms your deck—your cabin is as warm as though it had a stove going, but you feel quite cut off from that distant shrouded land that you can hardly see. You know from experience that it is a lovely summer day there, and people are complaining a little of the heat, but out here you are alone in the dominion of the southwest wind. You zip your coat tighter at the neck and change hands on the tiller. The cold is like a force against you. The land is far, far away. But all is well, the boat hasn't varied her angle or speed for hours. Once you pass a sloop running with spinnaker —at first a shadow far ahead, then white in the sun, then an actuality quite close, yawing and surging along with a lazy relaxed motion, and with people lying about in sunbathing attitudes—they wave almost reluctantly, as though with effort; and for the minute of passing her reality is somewhat astonishing, the white paint of the sides, the green bottom dipping and rising, the orange decks—you are fascinated by her ease and indolence as she weaves and rolls on the following sea: and those recumbent human beings—are they drugged by the wind and glare? Then she ceases to be real, is nothing but a white pyramid against the westering sunlight; she diminishes and diminishes to a point, a white speck against the whiteness of the eastern horizon.

You are cut off from everything again, but you begin to predict. Wind is still as steady as a cosmic force, but afternoon is waning, sun dead ahead, and as sure as night follows day your good southwest wind will weaken and fail. Old-timers say it heeds the tides—it comes in with the flood, dwindles with the ebb, but you don't take much stock in that. You guess, you hope, it will hold till sundown, and you figure on a harbor—in Maine there are good harbors always under your lee. You've been coming from Head Harbor, near Moose Peak; you have weathered Petit Manan, making good a steady five knots; you can't quite weather Schoodic Island—a hitch offshore again, past the whistling buoy, and with luck you can just fetch in the Eastern Way and make Northeast Harbor. Nothing better than that. And the wind, the good wind—will it hold, or will it leave you wallowing in calm off East Bunker Ledge?

In the late afternoon distances grow a little clearer. You see the mountains across Frenchman's Bay, dark, smoky gray, with strong shadows from the declining sun; you see more sails, a cluster of them like white flakes far up the bay beyond the islands where the water is slate blue. Wind is easier now, and when at last you come into the smoother waters off Seal Harbor, inside East Bunker Ledge with its stone beacon like a white sail, you feel the warmer air from the big islands to windward. The diurnal cycle is repeating itself, the calm, the sea wind, the calm, and perhaps the land breeze again in the night and dawn. The breeze is carrying you gently now on a close reach past Sutton's Island, under the Bear Island lighthouse on your starboard hand, and a vast serenity has settled over sea and land. Sky grows more luminous; sunset fires glow along the west; distant land is darker and clearer; the edge of sea beyond the Eastern way is deep blue against a white sky. Your boat slips along with hardly a ripple, but slow now; you see the harbor, the fleet lying idly at anchor, the reflections of white hulls and dark shores; at the mouth your sails fall slack, swing inboard, and you drift in total silence, waiting for the last few breaths to float you along to the inner waters.

Once the cycle of the classic coastal day establishes itself you feel it will go on repeating without end. Boating people count on it and fit their plans to it. But of course

there are other days, and even other cycles. There are
humid dog days, hot inland, but foggy and murky on the
coast—frustrating days for sailors when the fog rolls in
and out without warning: not the sinister blowing fog of
the easterlies, but a lurking cotton-wool fog that smothers
the islands. There are days of the east wind too, with rains
and misery—sometimes in spring they seem to be there
for weeks. And storms: the word is a common verb in
Maine, and refers to hard southeast or northeast winds
and rain, or even sometimes to any rainy spell. "It's begun
to storm," they say. Or "She'll storm before night." The
storm usually comes and goes within a day or a couple of
days, though the traditional span of the major storm is
supposed to be three days: but I recollect very few storms
that maintain intensity for that long. Even in winter the
great blizzards and gales blow by—or blow themselves
out—in shorter time.

The most dramatic play of coastal weather is the northwester, the "cold front" that sweeps down out of Canada
with a rush of arctic air—welcome in summer everywhere
in the northeast, with its cool crystalline atmosphere and
its brilliance and its promise of good days to come. But
often the northwester that seems benign along shore, blowing away seaward on water as blue as paint, is fierce and
implacable for the sailor. It comes in long gusts, each
harder than the last; it funnels out of the deep estuaries and
churns the big expanses of the bays into an intense dazzle
of dark blue and silvery foam. The big ones go on sometimes for two days and two nights, gusting up to fifty
knots, specially from early autumn any time through to
late spring, and in winter the intensest cold of the year

comes with them, the zero days with powder snow blowing across the fields and the white arctic smoke on the surface of the waters. In Maine they call any wind, great or small, a breeze—and a forty- or fifty-knot northwester can be quite a breeze. There is an intensity to it that other winds don't have—perhaps the dry clear air carries some quality of northern grandeur with it, and the great gusts swoop down more fiercely than ordinary winds. At the start of a great northwester the pressure is usually quite low, but rising, and it seems to me that low pressure gives a feeling of tension and expectation. Perhaps my own feelings about northwesters are particularly intense because the boats I have been responsible for have always been in danger from them, and I wake in the night again and again to hear the blasting wind and the crackle and splash of breakers on the rocks, and in the clear starlight I can see the boats plunging at their moorings.

Often they strike without warning, sometimes with an opening burst or squall, sometimes with a slow build-up that seems at first quite benign. Perhaps a student of weather maps and reports can tell, or an old-timer with a sixth sense, but even the most watchful amateur can be caught.

I was caught once off Small Point in a moving wall of fog, and another time in a northwester that behaved with such innocence that I hardly recognized it until my mainsail tore in two. It was a fine warm summer morning in Casco Bay, warmer than usual, with the southwester setting in for its day-long blowing—at least I supposed it was, but I failed to read the signs carefully. The air had none of the cold open-water feel it should have had, and in the western haze thunderheads lurked: but in summer they are frequent over the hot inlands. The breeze was also fitful, unlike the true southwester. Very gradually it worked into the west, and off the Kennebec, running eastward, I had to jibe from starboard to port tack.

On that day I was sailing alone in my sloop *Festina Lente*, to give her the full name which is seldom used. Someone with ancestral pride once adopted the words as a family motto, and though he had no thought of sailing craft it is the exact phrase for them: Make Haste Slowly. If she had been slow, I might have kept the *Lente*, but she is (as boats go) fast, and has very little room for a long name on her stern, so *Festina* she normally is. And with a rising westerly right behind her she was almost at her speed limit. Also on that day I had a cruising companion, the slightly larger *Charmian*, now owned by my brother-in-law and manned by a crew of three (including my younger son whose desire at the time was to beat his old man). So there we were, a hundred yards apart, surging along across Sheepscot Bay with wind on the port quarter, working into the northwest, still what seemed to be a good sailing breeze, specially for an eastward passage. Off Boothbay it was a true northwester, with gusts that frothed white on the protected waters. Off Pemaquid it began to feel like a gale. A big yawl was working against it with jib and jigger and power. *Charmian* forged ahead; her bigger hull had slightly more potential speed. I could feel *Festina* rush ahead in a burst, humming and trembling with the power of the squall, and then the frustrating surge against dead water as the hull reached the physical limit of its speed. Beyond Pemaquid Muscongus Bay seethed with white water. We should have taken off sail—was it rivalry that kept us going? or the wild exhilaration of the speed? or the realization that handling sail in such a wind would be tough work? A slim-hulled boat will run as fast in a gale, and behave much more quietly, with small sail—though *Festina* at the time was steering as gently as she always did. At any rate, the mainsail tore right across, from the leach inward—that old cotton sail by Ratsey I had acquired at second hand, and admired very much. And by the kind of good luck a sailor expects but seldom gets, I lowered away and gathered it in on the first try—no stuck slides, no snarled halyard coil, no boom flinging out of control, no canvas slatting itself to tatters.

So, a full-dress northwester on an August day in the middle of Muscongus Bay. Forty knots, I suppose, though I prefer to say fifty. It had come almost stealthily, little by little, first a nice summer sou'westerly, then a fresh warm westerly, now a cold gale.

Charmian, seeing me in distress a couple of hundred yards behind, came on the wind in a smother of spray, paid off on the other tack, and her mainsail tore across exactly as mine had. They lowered at once, subduing the heavy gaff and heavier boom.

Both boats under jib now, easily manageable with wind abeam, heading northeast for Port Clyde. Their jib was new, mine as old as the main—but it held. Up past Franklin Island, dodging through channels—we went fast and easy, except that the breaking steep chop from abeam kept dowsing me with cold spray. *Charmian* held on up the long reach of the St. George River and came into Port Clyde the back way; *Festina* ran for the main southern entrance and then easily and smartly beat up the harbor under jib alone—I took pride in her performance.

So we made it to Port Clyde, but the wind whistled through Herring Gut right into the anchorage, and the crowded lobster boats all danced and bobbled at their moorings, and the problems of anchoring were many and serious—and before we were through one of *Charmian's* anchors had fouled on an old chain on the bottom, and I had ignominiously fallen overboard and was hauled out by my son, a sequence that gave him some satisfaction. These are the by-products and aftermath of a big wind (or breeze, to use the correct local term), specially one that gives you so little time to get ready. The chief aftermath for me consisted of seven hours of sewing, which is what the mainsail demanded. *Charmian* had another one with her.

But nothing in the world's lands or seas is more beautiful than the morning after a northwester has stopped most of its blowing. The air seems fresher than it ever has been before, and every substance near and far sparkles with life and color: water of intensest blue, sea foam a dazzle of light, cliffs, trees, headlands all new and shining, a few lingering piles of innocent cumulus in the sky over the northwestward land, and the great sea all serene stretching off southward to deeper and deeper blue, marking itself like a ruled line against the pale infinity of the sky.

Boatmen of all sorts, but sailors particularly, learn to watch for squalls, which I am told are fiercer in some of the hot lands farther south and west than they are in Maine. From the northeastern vantage point we hear of tornadoes in Kansas and white squalls in the Chesapeake,

and I think even Massachusetts Bay can be very fierce.
But they come everywhere in hot seasons, in Maine too,
and anyone who commands a boat must fear them. The
explosion of wind and rain can be more than anyone is
equipped to withstand. You can see that something is coming; the black clouds build up in the west like doom, and
thunder crashes. But often on the coast the attack is more
sudden than you can believe. When the wind is blowing
from the south, right against the mounting blackness, you
are beguiled into thinking that the menace will move away
northward—as sometimes it does. And in heat, with a
warm southerly blowing, there's a thick haze along the
land; you can't clearly see what is happening; you hear
far rumblings and assume they are off in the interior somewhere. The wind blows fresh; you are sailing well. But
then the westering sun disappears; darkness falls; you look
up and see a high purple-black wall above you in the sky;
the wind slackens quite suddenly—you'd better get in sail.
If you listen you can hear it coming—the squall on the
water, a snarling rush louder and louder—and you see the
line of visible wind coming at you, dark on the surface,
then white and foaming: and you'd better be as ready as
you can, with sails furled, hatches closed, everything lashed
and fastened, rain gear on. Before you can breathe twice
you are swept and battered by a solid force of wind and
rain and spray, with a terrible uproar of thunder and lightning. Your boat heels, leans to it, scoots bare-poled over
the seething waters, and you need a mile or so of sea-room
to maneuver in—though for a few minutes you can see
nothing but blowing water before your eyes. First wind,
then rain, then both as one substance, with lightning down

your backbone and thunder right over the masthead—and then almost as sudden easing, perhaps a return of daylight in the west and a sight of island shores and landmarks, perhaps a few minutes of spooky silence and the forked lightning and thunder now farther away in the northeast. Luckily squall winds are offshore and there's nearly always water to leeward. The first attack is the deadly one, and any delay in defending against it can be dangerous. Yet as often you can be fooled into unneeded precautions: black sky builds up, lightning strikes on the western shores, thunder blasts, the whole world seems poised on the edge of doom—wind dies, light darkens, and in the end nothing happens. Or the attack begins in harmless rain, with no explosion of wind—just a slow even advance, coming and coming until it lashes itself up into a real blow and perhaps turns into a so-called weather front and keeps on all night. The signal for squall winds, if it can be seen in the general murk, is usually a small line of low cloud, white and close overhead, like a roll of cotton batting, moving fast; when you see that you haven't much time left.

And the dry easterlies—who can understand them or predict them? They are rare in Maine, and unnatural and beautiful. The weather prophets often predict east or southeast winds, and as often the actual wind comes west of south; sometimes they predict east to northeast winds, but can they ever recognize the strange dry brilliance that sometimes—hardly once a summer—comes with such a wind? I remember one summer when it blew day after day, and the old coastal logic was reversed. You beat east and ran west, and east was up and west down. No fog or storm in those easterlies, no trace or memory of fog: sky cloudless, horizon so dark and sharp that the distant blue waves notched it cleanly, like the cutting edge of a saw. You could anchor in sea-facing coves normally wide open to the southwesterlies. You could run with everything set from Penobscot to Casco Bay.

Weather prophets—old style: everyone who lives by water knows his life depends on weather, and he does his utmost to understand it; some succeed better than others, and a veteran seaman is certainly more knowledgable than a landsman—he knows whatever signs there are in wind and sky, and he reads the glass and consults his knee joints, and he remembers almost subconsciously all the portents and changes in a lifetime of watching. To an outsider he seems to have the mystic wisdom of Merlin, but if he is candid with himself he knows he can be wrong as often as right. He comforts himself with the thought that the weather bureau people are as unreliable as he is—perhaps more so. It annoys him that they pretend such certainty, as though the weather were being arranged by official government decree; he notes that they are never repentant and seldom admit their mistakes—though he isn't likely to, either. A prophet of any kind grows touchy about his reputation. But weather, specially downeast weather, so far passes all understanding. No one is sure of it, neither the old salt with a rheumatic joint nor the head meteorologist in Boston. What it amounts to is drama—by the day, the week, the year; it achieves constant surprise and suspense, and beauty and terror; it beguiles with sweetness and repels with the fierceness of its realities. The Maine winter on the coast can be oppressive with the week-long northwesters and zero days and nights, or with northeasterly blizzards and great seas battering the offshore islands, or with a sort of twilight world of gray east winds and damp snow—and the coastal spring comes so reluctantly that it seems to be the time when old folk die, as though they had given up hope of the warm sun. But then comes June—and and for five months the Maine weather is full of all the charm and surprise of good drama: in fog and sun, heat and chill, foul and fair, it is a continuous adventure, with scenes of surpassing beauty succeeding one another from icy freshness of sunrise to the last dark flames of sunset. In foggy times your world turns mysterious, strange distant sounds haunt the air, you withdraw into yourself in secrecy; in storms you share the old legends of the sea, and remember the exploits of brave seamen; in fair weather you rejoice in the flashing brightness of sea and land, and you push off once again on your never-ending quest for adventure among the islands.

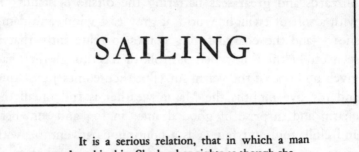

EIGHT

SAILING

It is a serious relation, that in which a man
stands to his ship. She has her rights as though she
could breathe and speak; and, indeed, there are
ships that, for the right man, will do anything but
speak, as the saying goes.

Joseph Conrad

THERE IS NO LONGER any sense or use to it. The sail,
like the horse and the ski, is vestigial. But all three
exist to save us from mechanism. They are the
remnants of a world now nearly lost—not the old transcendental world of the romantics, not quite. Salvation in
and by nature used to be the hope of older generations,
but the nature of an expanding universe grows more be-
wildering and more terrifying the more it is revealed. The
lovely harmonies of sea life and woodland life are little by
little receding, are being pushed away to the fringes—or
are being literally wiped out. Nature in the old-fashioned
sense must now be artificially preserved and set aside as a
recreational area, almost as though it were simply a large
arena designed for games. The salvation, if any, is merely
therapeutic; the greater truths lie elsewhere, in outer or
inner space.

Perhaps sails, like skis and horses, are no more than

recreational. They offer change and an unaccustomed activity and good appetites and healthy sleep. They allow for a release from the urban habits, for a certain kind of social display, for clothes, out-door tan, vanity. And the impact of beauty is genuine: blue sea, white hulls, curving sails—or perhaps mountains in winter. How lovely, how bright, how fresh the air! But the sailors may be protected by glassed shelters, with a motor to drive them home whenever they feel like it—and skiers of course require a million dollars worth of mountain development. The old primitive necessities become the organized pleasures of city people.

Yet much more must be said. A man who sails a boat is a captain. He decides, he acts; by his ability and nerve he surmounts danger, saves his ship and his crew, pits himself against the primordial powers of wind and water. He may take refuge in all available mechanical aids, but at bottom he is one with all the explorers and navigators who ever lived. He is, for the time at least, a man with a clear and compelling function. It can be a rare and salubrious experience in such a world as we live in.

He, the sailor, may be humorously aware of what game he is playing; he may confess his timidities and recognize himself as unsuited to the role of sea-rover—but none the less a boat under way, a tiller in his hand, a fresh southwest breeze and a horizon ahead, and he feels somewhere in his soul the response to the oldest of challenges. It happens to boys in sailing prams and old men in dinghies. And sometimes it happens so seriously and compulsively that a man will give up the rest of his life to it, as Captain Slocum did, and many others since: more now, in fact, than of old—at least more who are conspicuous single-handers, unable to resist the elemental challenge. In frontier times the challenge was a more normal part of a life's expectation.

And more must still be said. The ways of sailing are multitudinous. Every boat carries with it the connotations of centuries; it represents a world quite distinct from the land-world, with language and lore of its own, with techniques and equipment, knots, blocks, shackles, sheets, halyards, cringles, tacks, clews, gudgeons, luffs, roaches, leaches, garboards, dead-eyes, and with maneuvers and arts that became the symbols of man's conquest of both the world and his moral self. When you set forth across the harbor in a dory, say, with spritsail, centerboard, and steering oar, you are undertaking a little Homeric drama of your own, with the same stage and properties. As owner and master of a sailing craft you take on endless responsibilities: it is not simply a question of preserving yourself and friends from death by drowning, but of using your ship as she must be used, of maintaining her. A ship must be served, Conrad said. You must support her as you support a wife and family, with constant awareness of her welfare: does she need recaulking? or refastening? how are the keel bolts? the centerboard trunk? the rudder port? Are the garboards tight? is she weedy on the bottom? does she need burning off? how about the standing rigging? turn-buckles? splices? and the rest of the rig—you need a new mainsail obviously, and if you could move the whole thing six inches forward she'd steer better, but that would mean restepping the mast, resplicing the shrouds. . . . You need professional advice, perhaps, but you little by little live and talk and think in the classic world of the ship.

There's the performance too, the response to wind and weather, the handling, and the courses, maneuvering in channels, and harbors, anchoring and weighing anchor, the long runs offshore, the compass and log, the charts. And fog, what of fog? And squalls, gales. A small boat in a small area may represent innocence and security—to some degree it does: but the small boat is a perfect microcosm, nor do wind and weather temper themselves for the sake of the cautious. The sea's drama is always what it is.

Handling a sailing craft calls for practical competence: the seaman learns to hand, reef, and steer—and a great many other skills, though not as many for the fore-and-after as for the square riggers of old. The modern sailor need know nothing about box-hauling, for example, though the old trick of club-hauling might still come in handy off a lee shore (an early edition of Bowditch will discuss these and countless other maneuvers in the clearest kind of sea-man's language). But in our day sailing has no practical purpose. To take it seriously as a profession and way of life suggests evasion or irresponsibility, though no argument about duty can be pushed too far: a sailing craft is as good a place for contemplation as any, and the contemplative life has been much admired. Whatever its rating may be among serious thinkers, the sail does exist mainly as a recreation and sport, and the vast majority of its devotees are the young people who fanatically compete in yacht-club races. A very wholesome activity, and a test of competence and nerve.

Beyond all that, though, beyond the knowledge and the competence and the recreational delights, there is an experience in sailing that is beautiful in the same way that art is beautiful, particularly the art of music. In these times we talk big about art; it is what many serious people have instead of religion. When I was trying to learn to ski many years ago I remarked to a celebrated violinist that the techniques of skiing were more difficult than those of violining, and he was insulted. His art was sacred. Skiing was a sport for youngsters. All I had in mind at the time was "technique," but violins are played, Bach is played, *Hamlet* is played. Sometimes the play is for mortal stakes, as Frost said. At all events, there are moments when sailing a boat is purely an artistic pleasure, and sometimes the stakes are mortal. The word pleasure may destroy the truth I have in mind—at least for some it takes a low place in modern esthetics; but I use it hopefully.

For sailing as a true art you need first of all a good instrument—a good boat in other words and right there is where most failure occurs. The little boats are mostly good—better than they used to be, perhaps. Big boats are good, though bigness detracts. But middle-sized boats are designed to be big inside and small outside—at least a great many are, like the twenty-four footers that sleep four and the twenty-six footers that sleep six. The width and height provide room for bulky people, but the boat may look and behave like a sea-going bus. Every designer aims to achieve all things at once in his boat—speed, grace, sea-keeping ability, comfort, roominess, but it seems that the first essential in modern commercial design is to provide the largest possible amount of room in the shortest possible hull. The boat herself becomes a vehicle for water-camping.

One dreams often enough of the "good boat"—each man to his own taste. Mine is one that will sail. She moves easily and silently, as slick as a squid, as men say. She points high; she eats out to windward; she goes where she looks. She is long enough to go through an ordinary chop without bouncing, and she has enough flare and freeboard to be dry on deck. She is small enough to be handled alone, in and out of anchorages and channels, and she is very simply rigged, without the conveniences and equipment that weigh down some boats—I think specially of a sloop I have met here and there along the coast that is equipped like a floating boat show: her name is *Trouble*. The right size for a boat is thirty- to thirty-five feet overall, the right sail area less than four hundred square feet. Anything larger requires heavy anchors, heavy gear, and a serious semi-professional devotion. Anything smaller is likely to be wet, though many are fast and beautiful to sail. Very large boats are quite out of your hands; they may be splendid, like public monuments, but you are not in touch with them. So we dream of that swift and docile beauty that we can handle, be in tune with, feel the very breath and pulse of; we can drive her to windward all day, pointing higher, footing faster than anything in sight; we see how easily she slides along, how she balances, how gentle the weather helm is, how the foam and bubbles stream away along the lee rail, how flat the wake is. We keep alert to make sure that everything is going just right, like a harmony, like instruments in tune: an inch of sheet in or out can be felt through the whole complex fabric, a tremble of luff, a point up or off—are we pinching her a little? The sheet leads—are they just right? Angle of jib—the leach curls slightly, or does it? There may be back wind in the luff of the main. And the mainsheet traveler isn't really long enough; it pulls the boom in rather than down—the head of the sail sags off, trembles too much, You watch and listen and speculate; you let the jib sheet slip an inch; you luff her a moment and get the main in a half inch; you try to *feel* how she goes; you watch the bubbles sliding by the lee rail—faster now? It feels right, the momentum seems to have the right authority to it, the motion, the way she slices into the head sea; you check your course, the landmarks ahead, other sails—are you really outpointing that yawl a couple of miles to seaward or is it only your wish that makes it seem so? The tiller is so quiet in your hand yet you feel everything through it and you try to transmit your own will and desire to the boat; you urge her continually to be at her best. Your aim is to make everything work together in an ideal resolution and harmony of forces, sea, wind, hull, sails, and all the tensions of rope and wire and spars; you hope to achieve a sort of absolute of perfection, like the ultimate performance of a piece of great music.

Call it *allegro*, this going to windward in a whole-sail breeze, or *allegro vivace*: the rhythms are quick and at best joyous, the wind is fresh in your face, the wavetops flash silver ahead of you; the tall mast leans; sails are tight as drumheads but trembling with suppressed life, and she, your good boat, your lovely sentient fabric of wood and metal, drives and drives; the long bow thrusts and lifts and charges. You hear the note of wind in the wires, the tremor of the luff, the roll and swash of foaming water under the lee bow. You are in a way doing the impossible:

Festina Lente: call it *allegro*, this going to windward

you are charging full speed within three and a half points
of the wind's eye. You hardly understand what forces are
at work. What makes her *go*, you wonder—right up
against wind and wave. You know that everything counts,
from the top of her mast to the bottom of her keel; you
even know about the theory of sailing to windward, and
you know that it works, but the actuality of it is a wonder.
Every bit of her is under tension, the sheets, blocks, cleats,
the sailcloth—how can it endure? And the stays and
spreaders, the forty-foot mast tilting, all the turnbuckles
and shackles and eyebolts, and the hull itself, straining,
smashing, working; and the ton of lead down on the keel,
the long bolts up through the floor timbers. Yet on she
goes, hour after hour, doing what she was designed and
created to do.

The moods of sail can be very different: some are quiet
and pensive, some heavy, some very light. Running down-
wind in a light breeze is like a kind of dream: no sound, no
sense of motion, no feel of the air, yet the effect is of being
sustained in a void. Running with a strong breeze and a
following sea is the most uninhibited drama of all—perhaps in music it is the big brass band, or in skiing the full-
length down-mountain run. All is free and splendid. You
cheer; you shout with unpremediated joy; you feel Olympian. Let her go, let her go, let her *go*! Let her roll and
surge, let her carry the crest of a sea along like a surfboard.
And how sweetly she steers, how gentle and eager—how
the curling seas roll up behind her and seethe along right
under and away: how beautiful is the way of a good little
ship with the sea. You look back at the foaming waters
behind you, to windward, and ahead at the blue distances,

and you have an illusion of great power and command: this is the way we go round the world, you think; these are the Roaring Forties eastward of Cape Horn. This is the day you can break all records—here we go for Boone Island, Cape Elizabeth, Monhegan, down East all the way.

But for pure sustained elegance nothing is like a reach. Wind abeam, smooth waters, sails full and easy, boat steady—and then the speed, the unbroken rush, seven knots. Hull speed, they call it. As fast as the hull will go. An easy tiller (if you have the right boat), lay it gently on your knee, lean back, enjoy the scene, pick out your buoys and marks far ahead, and watch her run. There'll be a roll of foam under the bow and a gurgle of wake aft as she hits her speed limit, but more noise will come from the tender (if you are towing one). Perhaps you can adjust the painter so the tender will ride on the down slope of the second wave in your wake—you have a notion it tows easier that way. In Maine there are Reaches, so named: Moosabec and Eggemoggin, each about ten miles; and in the summer southwest wind you can reach either way, east or west. The water is smooth; the wind freshens in across the seaward islands, and a sailing craft can make wonderful knots. Reaching is the picture-book aspect of sailing, the almost too delightful part of it, the long, straight, easy coast.

These are some of the pleasures of sailing, and they give the illusion of controlled and beautiful harmony—or perhaps "art" is the better word, if we aren't too serious about it. But what if chance and reality break in, as they must? What if the wind blows too much, or not at all? It is the risk we take; it can be serious, or even mortal. Any ship, great or small, can be controlled up to a point, but after that desperation sets in. There is no restraint to wind and sea, no limit to what they can do: sails tear, rigging breaks, masts break, hulls are swamped or smashed—or the man himself fails, mishandles his boat, mistakes his course, and all harmony is destroyed. Perhaps the ever-present threat is what makes the beauty of sailing so intense; round about us is the threat of chaos, but here with good luck and good skill we achieve the form and meaning we always seek. Like a composer and conductor we are for the time being very like a god.

There are the ironies of perfect calm too, when the ship with all her fine prospects is impotent; she drifts and turns like flotsam, perhaps for hours—in rain, perhaps, or hot sun. Today's boatmen switch on the power and charge along to their destination, but the old reality of sail includes the calms, and the patient waiting for change, sometimes the most intense frustrations. Yet the sailor, if he takes pleasure in the whole experience of it, learns to be artful in calm; he watches the catspaws and currents, the waft of distant smoke—he gains a few yards with a sense of minor triumph; he works her along from air to air—slow enough, but what is speed in sail? In remote Sargasso Seas ships may have lost themselves for ever, but here along the coast the breeze will come again; the long noon stillness will change to the onshore airs of afternoon. The worst part of a windless sea is the pitch and roll, when sails and spars slam back and forth and there's no escape. But among islands the water is smoother and the air often stirs through the channels and on the lee side of trees, and if you make no appreciable progress in the end you can anchor and go ashore and walk on shady beaches.

The question is how serious we can be about all this—whether we think of it as a pleasure, an art, or a way of squandering life. Sailing is also a social recreation. Families go off for outings and overnight cruises. You invite friends; you take out parties. Someone steers, and whether she points high or low, luffs or falls off, is of no consequence. You are all afloat; it is a fine day; sea air is fresh; conversation is brisk—there go the Watsons, there go the Sterlings, and whose is the new house on the point? They love your boat, the color of the deck, the cushions, the sails—are they Dacron or nylon or what? Your rival comes along, tuned to perfection, outfoots and outpoints you—a lovely boat, they all say; see how she goes. The wind freshens, lee rail goes under, but they all are good sports, they laugh and hang on—but we'd better turn back, we can relax better on an even keel; talk is brisk again, day is fine, air is fresh.

Perhaps the serious musician is a bore too. No chatter for him, no idle enthusiasm for the recreational pleasures of pretty music. All is austere and high and somehow beyond the grasp of everyone else. The serious sailor can be more nearly obsessed than almost any other specialist, particularly the one who competes, who devotes his life and money to racing, who lives wholly in a vision of ultimate efficiency and ultimate speed under sail. Perhaps he loses some of what we ordinarily think of as sanity, and very probably he grows arrogant or at least impatient with the innocence and ignorance of others. Great enterprises of all kinds, great visions, great art, great excellence, play havoc with human nature, destroy balance, create fantastic dreams of success and failure, eliminate the humility and the humor and the kindness that in the end save men from themselves. But sailing a boat still remains one of the great enterprises, rooted as it is in man's nature, in his history and culture, and developed in the long trials and errors of time to the perfection of the present-day yacht.

NINE

THE GOOD SAILOR

Of all the living creatures upon land and sea, it is ships alone that cannot be taken in by barren pretences, that will not put up with bad art from their masters.

Joseph Conrad

A widower with two boys asked for advice on bringing them up and was told to get them a boat and teach them to sail. Any advice is risky, and this took the risk of turning the boys into vagabonds. Some who set off in boats never come back. But a boy in charge of a sailboat is taking the basic course in survival, with credits in patience, ingenuity, responsibility, and other fringe studies. He may for a while despise everything else, but the kind of self-reliance he gets from handling his boat is what we generally think well of, specially in a world dedicated to whatever is convenient.

Not, perhaps, the plastic boat, the yacht-club one-design that is raced every Wednesday and Saturday with forty others exactly like it—though even that has much to commend it. But a boy may share in his boat's destiny. It is a kind of trial marriage: he supports her in sickness and health; he is responsible for her whole welfare, her fastenings, caulking, paint and varnish, the smoothness of her bottom, the cut and trim of her rig, all the details of her deportment. He sees to her moorings, bails her out after rains, secures her in storms, wakes in the night to wonder if all is well with her. He sees to her hauling out and her storage in winter and all the labors of getting her ready in spring and launching her and rigging her—and perhaps he decides it isn't worth it, the time and devotion; he must earn money, pursue a career, be serious about life.

These idle habits of boating and sailing are so woven into the fabric of my life that they have fixed the pattern. I can row and paddle and scull as easily as I can walk, a condition common in coastwise people, of course. The most skillful oarwielder of my experience is the Venetian gondolier, whose technique is more demanding than it looks—and one time years ago I tried it in spite of the emotional objections of the gondolier. The single oar is a heavy ten-footer, bent at an angle near the middle, and it rests, not securely in a lock, but on a very small ledge on a stand rising a couple of feet above the after deck: the oar is free to slip backward, a necessity in the narrow ways— and when it slips backward it falls from the stand and trails behind. The thirty foot gondola, keelless, sits on the water like a long dish and must be moved on a straight course by this long heavy oar wielded from the after deck. Anyone at all used to small boats can see how impossible the problem is: the tricks of sculling and paddling and rowing are all combined into a single movement which is constantly thwarted by the oar's falling away from the precarious stand it is supposed to thrust against. A dedicated boatman would, or should, observe these details, but I have never seen them in print, nor have I ever met any outsider like me who has propelled a gondola down the Grand Canal. I thought I did well, but I wouldn't have lasted twenty feet in one of the little canals. To watch a native master at work is a revelation for any boatman.

I always assume I can handle anything with a sail on it, though my ways are probably those of the whimsical amateur. There are masters and supermasters of sail, as in all major enterprises of humanity. The great racers and world cruisers are celebrated: to achieve the ultimate skill in sailing, unceasing competition is required—week after week of racing with no quarter asked or given. It too is a life in itself—a specialized one. There are fleets and clubs everywhere, even on the coast of Maine, where able sailors devote their hearts and minds and bodies wholly to the twice-a-week race. But my sailing mostly calls for solitude and a contemplative habit. Often I do it alone, and being alone makes a kind of challenge.

The master, Joshua Slocum, had a very heavy boat, and by modern standards a very awkward one. Gaff mainsail, solid long spars, thick canvas, halyards and sheets with many blocks and double blocks. Anchors too heavy for a man to lift. How could he handle her through the world's storms and squalls, on the most desperate seas, and in and out of crowded ports? He came into Gloucester under full ·sail on a windy day and brought up snug and safe at a wharf—he called it luck, but he did it. He weathered tidal waves off Africa and williwas in the Straits of Magellan. Luck partly—you have to have it. Strength, in his case: his physical endurance seems to put him up with the heroes of epic and fable, though he took it for granted as the expected equipment of any seaman. He spent his life heaving and hauling the solid gear of big and little ships, and could do it with the slow stoic patience of a professional. More than strength, he had the kind of patience that goes best with natural events; he could wait and wait for things to happen in his favor, and hours and days were never in themselves worth saving. Like the creatures of earth and sea he was never driven by the delusion of time wasting. The hardest ordeal of the modern sailor is to accept the rhythm of the forces he has to use and deal with; a man in a sailing craft must wait for time and tide, and if he reconciles himself to the natural cycles he can be serene inside and can in the end achieve what he thinks of as his goal. It was a way more prevalent in Slocum's day than ours. Darwin took five years for his great voyage, and behaved as though he had all eternity at his disposal.

The schooners of those days were the very emblems of patience. They rode at their anchors in the many harbors of Maine waiting forever, it seemed—sometimes with mainsail set all night and all day in the wayward airs, perhaps while the fog rested on the islands; and often when they finally stirred and the chains clanked in through the hawseholes the process was as slow as something in a dream, and ships and men seemed to be fixed in a kind of general hypnosis.

The lone sailor can afford to overlook nothing. As far as his life and activity at sea go, he is one on whom nothing is lost. He must never be absent-minded, or in any small way careless. With practise the concentration becomes part of his nature—he may even be able to contemplate

truths other than those of wind and water, but some fraction of his mind must be continually concerned with every
detail of whatever is happening. He watches the large expanses of his world for signs, the clouds, smokes, surfaces
of water, fogs, the look of far objects, and he feels every
shift and vagary of moving air, but he also sees the frayed
lanyard and the unraveled rope's end and he notes that his
halyard coil is askew, his anchor on deck is three or four
inches off line and may snag the jib sheet. Or he notes that
in his hurry to set the jib he belayed the halyard with a
half hitch on the cleat that might take up two extra seconds
in casting off, and while he aims to handle his boat with
plenty of seconds to spare he knows that there are moments
when two seconds can spoil a planned maneuver such as
anchoring in a congested harbor—he remembers the time
he had to get in sail fast, let it drop in a sudden heap on
the boom (as a good sail should), and a little length of
nylon lashing whipped itself round the halyard: why was
it there? and why hadn't he noticed it? and why should it
choose this one time in the infinity of time to tangle into
a running halyard? A few seconds to undo it, and the sail
caught a veering puff, filled, the boat swung the wrong
way, and there he was all messed up in billowing cloth
and snarled halyards, fending off from moored boats, be-
having in all ways like the incompetent amateur he was
trying not to be.

In the handling of boats there are infinite opportunities
to do the wrong thing; there are also infinite ways in which
your luck can be bad. Fittings that have held up for years
suddenly break. Anchors foul on old chains. Squalls
pounce. Uncharted rocks loom under you. The natural

forces are too much for you. Or your vulnerable flesh and bones give way and leave you impotent. Yet one of the signs of the good sailor is that his luck is always good—or nearly always. Slocum was lost in the end—he vanished from the seas and was seen no more, and in a dramatic sort of way it seems appropriate; he went heroically, after a lifetime of victories. He had had much bad luck too, in his earlier days—he was troubled in spirit and mortal; but in the great period of single-handed voyaging he not only did everything right, he triumphed over bad luck itself. The good sailor tries to make everything happen in his favor, and of course he watches for everything, anticipates and out-guesses—he suspects the chain on the bottom, or the unmarked rock, the faulty metal; he is as alert to possibilities as any wild creature whose life is forever in danger. But if he is good at it he has few adventures to report: all generally goes well, and he returns from far places with what outwardly seems the greatest of ease.

The bad sailor is continually persecuted by nature and chance. His food and water go bad; his sails blow out; his vessel leaks; winds are against him—everything that can go wrong does so. In the end he comes home and writes a book, and perhaps he thinks himself heroic in his survival —or at least he congratulates himself on withstanding all the bad luck that attacked him. He has much to tell and may write a fine book. But it is true that bad luck clusters round incompetence. Any ship's captain knows that his employers require him to have good luck and that any failure, no matter what the cause, will count against him. Even if at night he runs into a floating mine left over from an old war, he is somehow responsible: the ship was his to preserve, and the damage is done under his command.

Once some years ago three young men were cruising eastward through the Deer Isle Thoroughfare, following along from buoy to buoy in the well-marked channel, leaving red to port and black to starboard. A beautiful clear evening, with a dying west wind and a setting sun flaming up into the western sky. All seemed serene. The young men were filled with happiness. Nothing in all life could be better or more beautiful than this time and place. But it was getting late and they were hungry, so the one who was captain in an informal sort of way turned the helm over to another and went below to cook supper. He got the stove going and was browning a pan of roast beef hash; the boat was as steady and even as a room ashore, all was very quiet except for the little whisper of the burning stove, and he was relaxed on a stool with his back against the mast. He could see the crimson western sky in the frame of the companionway. What happened then is what every boatman dreads more than anything else. The solid smash against rock. No warning or suspicion, no noise or signal, just the impact of iron against granite: five tons stopped—five tons that had been slipping along about as fast as a man could walk. A falling tide—and you'd be apt to say "of course." Bad luck acts that way. And there was the black can buoy, well to port, the wrong side.

Violent activity by the crew of three. Anchors rowed out, tackle to masthead (jib halyard, no doubt), boat hove down to reduce draught, and then hauling and heaving and swaying—all to no avail. A five-ton boat on a ledge in a falling tide stays there. A deep-keeled boat lies way over on her side, the position can be dangerous, she might roll down, slip off a ledge. Other dangers loom up, wind, any sea making up, unknown damage.

A long anxious night ahead. The proud sloop high and dry, ignominiously lying on a weedy ledge at a forty-five degree angle. And the happy crew turned grim, finding fault, assigning blame.

But luck worked both ways. The night stayed as still as glass. No timbers were crushed or started. Tide flooded so gently that no one knew the moment she floated and swung to the anchor—and all that had happened had been in darkness. In the morning light she looked as free and proud as she ever did. But the young captain knew whose fault it was. Down there cooking hash, ruminating on the serenity of the, evening and the pleasures of cruising, he had no thought for that black can on the port side. He took everything for granted, and was beguiled by the security of the quiet ship.

It is an axiom among sailors, as well as others, that if anything can go wrong it will. If there is a mathematical possibility of say one in ten thousand that a certain shackle will let go, it not only will, but will do it quite soon. If you moor or anchor your boat in a cove open to the west you tell yourself that westerly gales almost never occur in Maine, and on a calm summer evening the possibility is too unlikely to think about: that's what fooled young Ben Carrick when he first launched his sloop and put her on the old mooring in Carrick's Cove. The westerly gale blew her ashore. It is true also that a sailing vessel, large or small, can get herself into the kind of mess that passes all belief, and can do it quickly and spitefully: she resents bad handling; she is merciless in exposing incompetence; the more you try to control her the more cussed and contrary she gets. Getting an anchored boat under way in a crowded harbor takes exact planning and timing, and perhaps an expert does it so quietly you take no notice of him—you see him scudding out the harbor mouth with all sail set as though he had simply pushed off and let her go. But suppose your mainsheet snarls, you come off on the wrong tack, your anchor breaks out and drags, your jib billows up suddenly and envelopes you in yards of cloth; you fight your way out, drop the anchor line and run back to unsnarl the sheet and put the helm over, run forward to grab anchor line again, run to lee rail to fend off from the blue yawl whose enamel finish is already gouged, run aft to clear your sheet from the yawl's stanchions where it has tied itself up in three or four half hitches, run forward to get your jib out of the water . . . all this so far is just an effort to put yourself in a position where you can start over again; but meanwhile you have no steerage way; your anchor is still out there but perfectly useless—it must be fouled, you suppose, and now you drift backward with your sail slatting like a battery of drums and your boom swinging wildly—sooner or later it will crash into your head, you know it will, you expect it to, you might as well cry out in advance like the White Queen; and, of course, there are ranks of moored boats, some with bowsprits leveled at you like bayonets, and all the population of the harbor stops whatever it is doing and watches you and begins to shout advice. Your boat, your old friend and mistress and wife that you have loved and cherished these many years, is suddenly possessed, she is malevolent and menacing, the great sail is full of power, the dead weight

under you is more than you can manage, she won't do anything you want her to do, she seems even to take a kind of
malicious pleasure in finding new ways to make trouble.

Theory in the crises of sailing helps very little. The
complicated temperament of a boat has to be discovered
and learned in endless practice, and the infinite chances of
wind and water. The large traditional maneuvers may
seem clear enough, but the oddities and accidents are never
the same, the jammed block or the torn cringle, the lee or
weather helm, the distance she will or won't carry steerage
way, the kind of sail she needs in different conditions,
what makes her good-natured or ill-natured, or lovable or
hateful. Once long ago I watched a small fishing sloop
beating against wind and tide at the eastern end of Moosabec Reach, bound for Jonesport and home. He had been
handlining and had fresh fish aboard; he hoped to get into
the Reach before the tide turned, but the day-long breeze
began to fail, the flood began to make, and here he was—
first a starboard tack toward Mark Island, than a port tack
to the mouth of Chandler's Bay, back and forth, gaining
foot by foot—up to the narrows where current ran harder.
He was an hour too late; his luck was bad. Each tack at
last brought him to the same spot, again and again. A
rather sad little sloop with a long boom and a peak that
sagged and an ineffective little jib, but she had none the
less the proud clipper bow of the so-called Friendship
model. Finally he began to lose rather than gain. He walked
forward, took off his cap with a marked gesture, and
kicked the mast for all he was worth. He wore boots, and
failed to damage either himself or the mast, but with each
kick he told her what he thought of her—his voice sounded

out over the flowing tide. Then he eased her over toward a spot of land called Virgin Island and anchored.

I speak all along of the pure sailing craft. She requires a certain temperament. If you are one who kicks and curses, she is not suitable for you. Among old-timers that Jonesport fisherman was a rarity, though I suppose what I saw that evening was no more than a lover's quarrel: it happened that the boat I sailed made it through the narrows where his didn't, and his anger was understandable. But sailors had to learn infinite patience. Few remain, actually. The modern craft is a prefabricated package designed to eliminate all the traditional frustrations; she is meant to work almost as easily as an automobile, with a switch for lights, a switch for engine, and winches on every sheet and halyard, depth finder, direction finder, no leakage, no rust, no paint to blister. The habits of ease are irresistible. All skippers resort to power at every hazard—the narrow windward channel, the crowded anchorage, the fog run, the drawbridge, any long beat to windward: does anyone in these times beat the fifteen miles from Wiscasset to open water? Sailing craft used to work through the high-tide channels of the Mt. Desert Narrows, now blocked forever by the highway. In Boothbay Harbor I saw a cruising schooner beautifully rigged and equipped and ready for anything—except that she had no main sheet. You shouldn't try going east without power, they say; tides and fogs and other hazards offer too much danger for sail alone. But the trouble isn't danger, it is impatience, time pressing, the importance of getting somewhere. Any sailing craft is an anachronism, but the pure and essential sailing craft is so absolute an anachronism that we keep her on hand only for competitive purposes, like the show dog and the race horse; she becomes beautiful, but very specialized and impractical.

The sailor is looking for freedom and a safe way to get back to the primitive—not too safe, though; the nettle of danger must be real enough. The sea remains great and powerful; his boat is very small and alone. In spite of the navigational conveniences he fares forth in tne spirit of Magellan and Cook: horizons, landfalls, shoals, breaking seas—all are unchanged since the beginning of time; all are there to be faced with skill and boldness. He, like the legendary ones, is on his own. He believes in his will, in his power over his own destiny—he must, or he wouldn't be there, nor would he survive. The command is his; success or failure depends on what he can do, and all the problems of life are simplified and clarified. He knows that he is in the hands of chance, and of all the infinite forces surging over and about him—he knows how helpless he may in the end be, but meanwhile he accepts the responsibility. He knows that good sailors in the past have challenged bad luck,' angry gods, and implacable nature, and have achieved victories. Perhaps he knows that it is all illusion, like any other game that men play to beguile themselves, but he can't ask more than that—not if he is wise.

TEN

CRUISING

Only the young have such moments. I don't
mean the very young. No. The very young have,
properly speaking, no moments. It is the privilege
of early youth to live in advance of its days in all
the beautiful continuity of hope which knows no
pauses and no introspection.

Joseph Conrad

YOU BEGIN WITH A BOAT, and in this day, when comfort is the supreme good, boats are much more
luxurious and elaborate and expensive than they
used to be. My father's boat, which he bought new for
five hundred dollars, was what used to be called a knockabout, a low-sided, long-ended twenty-eight footer, with
flat spoon bow, broad stern, jib and gaff mainsail, and
cabin space with a flat floor and three feet of headroom. He
and my mother cruised in her for many summers, and my
brother and I for many more. In the cabin if you sat on
the floor your head brushed the beams of the roof. All
supplies, stoves, pots, plates, and such equipment were
carried in wooden boxes, some of which had to be put
out in the cockpit at night to allow room for sleeping. The
toilet was a bucket, awkward in the cabin, more convenient
to use on the foredeck next the mast. The boat herself could
be very fast, faster than most boats of her size today, but

she was lightly built and in my time very leaky, both below and above. After a hard beat to windward the bedding was always wet and water sloshed across the floor boards. But what delight to sail her! She could ghost along on no breeze at all. She was responsive and eager—and though she pounded in a head sea she stood up and drove into it bravely.

Old people always make much of the primitive delights they remember out of their past. In my day, they say, we had wonderful pleasures—the buggy rides, the hay wagons, the camping in wild country, the sailing and cruising in knockabouts: and on the whole I think they are right. It was a simpler, sweeter, wilder world. Mystery hovered over it, the old transcendental ecstasy of Wordsworth or Thoreau where even the simplest natural area offered infinite surprises and glimpses of the unknown. The difference is not only in the mechanization, but in the loss of all that the word "frontier" connotes. Beyond the Missouri lies—what? Once an infinity of unknown wildness; now highways and motels. The rational mind must accept it. Romantic mystery is for children—and even children learn better very early. What the young expect is a camp ground with plumbing and sites allotted by an attendant, or a ski area developed into lifts and heated pavilions, or sailing administered by a yacht club with age-group programs. Mechanization and population—there is no escape and no end. The young are already in it, geared to it, perhaps happy about it—or at least complacent. The word "modern" means good and desirable.

I suppose I was brought up in the Indian summer of transcendentalism. Wild places were not merely pleasant vacation spots, but represented the mystery of God. If the sound of a waterfall in spring haunted the young Wordsworth like a passion, so did the sound of surf on a rocky coast haunt me. My mind was full of the visions of the wild outer coast of Isle au Haut, the most sublime and godly place, I thought, in the world. The experience of being there was one of exaltation.

This is all a matter of record rather than opinion or protest. The prison of the world, as the poet said, does close upon the growing boy. The prison of the rational mind closes too—or perhaps it is more just to say that the rational mind deprives us of the dreams and illusions that once filled us. Man's destiny is to accept facts, do away with illusions, master nature, utilize power. It is also to propagate and multiply.

Sailing in a primitive little boat along what I took to be a wild and primitive coast was the purest delight of my life. I think the same delights are sought for today, but I have not met with the same simple-minded ecstasy. The boats are now as efficient as their corresponding vehicles ashore, the automobiles. All things are better, stronger, more efficient, and the sailor is safer and easier in mind and body. He can move from port to port almost on a schedule, as he might drive so many miles a day on land. The only troubles he has are likely to be mechanical ones: the engine overheats, the batteries don't charge—and he stops at ports where gasoline and oil and spare parts are supplied and good mechanics are available. It is an irresistible force, this increasing mastery of the primitive, and we are almost helpless in its grip. In any community of boats few row with oars, any more than they walk from one place to another, and in general few sail in the face of difficulty such as too much or too little wind. Except for the racers, of course, who invent and face up to difficulties as a sort of backlash against the insidious pleasures of comfort.

Nor is there the same sense of remoteness that there used to be. All is discovered and known—even the secret headwaters of Little Kennebec Bay which once seemed like a small heart of darkness wholly remote from any known world, where only herons and bitterns and hawks flourished among forests and swamps. Not long ago I groped in a fog into the mouth of Dyer's Bay, another remote water running in a long way from Petit Manan Point, and the first object I sighted was a moored seaplane. Perhaps the notion of undiscovered regions has been for a long time a delusion. The heart does cloud the mind. The coast was charted long ago. More people lived there a century ago, and old records speak of the fleets of vessels —fifty sail, say, getting under way off Boothbay Harbor after a change of weather. But even discounting the sentiment and nostalgia, that wondrous quietness of old times did once exist as a reality, and the communities lived apart like independent little countries, and you could browse among eastern islands forever, it seemed, without being reminded of any outside world.

East of Schoodic: to any young cruiser of earlier times that was the beckoning mystery. All sailing people knew about Mount Desert and the waters off Northeast and Bar Harbors: eastward lay the long point of Schoodic, with its mountain headland, and the wild island outside, and beyond all that the unknown. No resorts or yachts, not even any names familiar in legends and books—except perhaps Petit

Manan, and far off like an ominous echo the splendid Grand
Manan. Machias—one had heard of it. And Jonesport and
Moosabec Reach, and last of all Eastport.

A boy's thoughts and dreams, but any cruising is made
of similar stuff. Some boys sail round the world. I made it
to Eastport. A small venture, but sustaining for much of
a lifetime, and still graphic in my mind so that though I
have been down that way many times since then my vision
of eastern Maine has the look and color of that early
discovery.

I had the little knockabout, named *Bettina*, not very
well taken care of, though I loved her as a boy must love
his boat; but I was unable to cope with her leaks and minor
weaknesses of character. She was never intended for serious
cruising, but she was always beguiling, and I have regretted
ever since that I didn't know enough to take better care
of her. I enlisted a companion, and we started eastward in
fine weather, with supplies and bedding heaped and secured
in a pile in the middle of the cabin floor, wedged against
sliding by a long oar on one side and a spinnaker pole on the
other. Our last port in the known world was Southwest
Harbor, where we lay quietly in a cloud of mosquitoes. In
the morning the hum and whine of a smoky sou'wester,
brief debate as to a reef in the mainsail—no reef, and away
we went due east. *Bettina* had a flat, wide hull like a fruit
dish, and in a following or quartering wind she surged
dizzily along on the surface, rushing and planing on wave
crests—pulling very hard on her helm but making wonderful speed. That was one of her great days. Jonesport in
seven hours. A grand rush into the unknown. Schoodic
under our lee, the smoky and foamy waters of Petit Manan

A grand rush into the unknown

where mariners are told to beware, beware! Rips and
shoals and breaking seas on the bar—worst in a sou'-
wester like this where the sea wind meets the ebb full tilt.

On any day such as this, with the smoke-white haze
over land and sea, you feel remote and alone. The coast is
visible as a gray blur, with barriers of surf and off-lying
ledges: no houses, no boats, no glimpse of anything man-
made—except only the incredible gray shadow in the
white sky that you identify as the lighthouse tower of
Petit Manan. An apparition, so unnatural and ghostly that
it strikes you with fear, though it marks your course for
you: it is too tall, too solitary, too wild—how can it stand
in a rage of wind and sea, out among those breaking shoals?
You feel more lonesome because of it, more cut off from
the world: if you could see it plainly, you think, it might
be a comfort, but it is misty and dreamlike. But then you
are surging over the bar, the shallow passage between the
mainland and the cluster of ledges that make up Petit
Manan itself, and your boat spins and rushes like a canoe
in a spring flood—but she is buoyant and light, she stays on
top of it, she and her towing tender come through.

And there you are in new and strange waters, running
east by north, past Jordan's Delight and Shipstern Island,
heading for Cape Split. The cruiser gets used to that solitude. Even a day's run along the coast cuts him off from
mankind. His reality is his little ship, and the circle of
visible water. In time he welcomes it, puts his trust in the
ship and his own competence. Captain Slocum seemed to
have no fear of the remotest solitudes.

On that day Jonesport loomed in the mists like a
frontier town, an ugly fish-factory place strewn along the

shore of Moosabec Reach with houses like toy blocks painted green and yellow and a tide-scoured waterfront and a few spindly wharves. No shelter for a small boat, except for a cove too shallow to get into: the wind whistled across the width of the Reach and the tide rushed like a river. We rounded to in the mouth of Sawyer's Cove near a couple of sloops and a lumber schooner, anchored in a bobble of windy water, furled sails, snugged down, and realized how incongruous we were in our flimsy little white yacht off here on the rugged northeastern frontier. It might have been Labrador, by the look of things—or so we thought in our summer innocence.

But I think we were not far wrong. Modern power had just begun to come to the remoter ends of the coast: Jonesport existed by itself, miles from railroad or highroad; sails and oars were still in use, though the herring boats that supplied the packing plant were gasoline powered. In the half century since then the great changes have come, but whether for ultimate good or ill I can't tell. The ugliness remains.

I had had enough experience by then to know that good cruising depends on good eating—by which I mean eating in quantity. One burner, a Swedish primus, set on the cabin floor, will effectively heat soup, beans, tomatoes, and cocoa in order—and that's the way it was. With a can of peaches to follow. More modern comforts can do better, specially in providing ice and a broiler, but true innocence and hunger make no such demands. It would be impossible to conceive of greater happiness than ours at the eating of our soup, beans, tomatoes, cocoa, and peaches—with cookies from home. Cruising goes best in youth, of course.

Too tall, too solitary, too wild—how can it stand in a rage of
wind and sea?

Ashore to buy mosquito netting, to see the town—even to go to a play: a traveling company appearing in *Way Down East* in a hall with kerosene lamps and no footlights, a melodrama of the Uncle Tom era, not a revival or a jest but a solemn remnant of the nineteenth century, with histrionics on the stage and silence in the audience. A small audience, I think.

That night fog, rain, thick weather. Leaks, drips, damp bedding; cotton pads hard and thin on the wood floor. Boom of distant foghorns, mystery of a strange wild coast. But you lie warm, and all of life is concentrated on this place and moment; you are almost hypnotized by the detachment of it: here you are, warm, motionless, safe, while all round is infinite rain, fog, unknown regions of danger. It is a state of mind well known to the cruiser, and sometimes renders him impotent: the little cabin is as still and quiet as a burrow or a grave, better snuggle down, stay put, wait. . . . Is she dragging? Is she in shoal water? Will it blow straight in on you—perhaps work up to some sort of gale? And those twenty foot tides you have heard about—have you got scope enough? The thoughts drift in your mind—you push them away, you doze and dream, you are warm, steamy warm, a cocoon. The hours pass, daylight, morning, noon. There you are, under a spell. The foghorn goes on and on from a great and lonely distance.

Then change, a new scene. You see a cloud moving, west to east, a tatter of blue. Suddenly an unbearable impatience seizes you: fair wind coming, a clear horizon. You struggle with clothes, blankets, food—hurry, hurry, shredded wheat, scrambled eggs, bread, jam, no time to boil coffee—wash up later. West wind now, northwest wind, breaking clouds—ominous looking, hard blow probably coming. But stow everything, pump out (always pump out), up sail, up anchor, away in a rush, leaning to it, paying off, jibing, whizzing past deserted old sloops and schooner (waiting for a westward chance), away eastward into the unknown, wind hard over the port quarter, dark clouds piling down from the northwest—but shafts of sun now, and dazzles of white. The sea ahead all purplish and silver—the mystery of Englishman's Bay and Machias Bay and the white shaft of Libby Island Lighthouse against an ink-blue sky behind it. Away, away! She planes along, the new land wind whitens the dark waters, islands, ledges, buoys come and go—no need to worry about tide current in this wind. Seven knots, sea still smooth but building up to a steeper chop. Roque Island to windward—famous place, come to think of it, famous beach: can't stop now, must go with the strong fair wind, heading east. But a lonely world—nothing in sight, no boat or house in any direction, except the white shaft of Libby Island. Strange how ominous a solitary lighthouse seems, as though it warned you not to be there—and you knew how incongruous your toy boat was against this stormy coast.

But you hold eastward, keeping her off with a steady hard pull on the tiller—rolling your easting down, as you say to yourself, pretending to be on a great voyage. Beyond Machias Bay the coast is wilder, more lonely, the cliffs higher. You close in under its lee, with wind in puffs. The shore looms above you like a mountain range. No habitation anywhere, but the chart shows a harbor, a lighthouse, bell buoy—you hold on eastward, watching the seamarks, aware of the wildness of the region: and then a sudden opening of a little bay, a white tower and bellhouse snug against an almost black forest, and the quiet water of a narrow harbor and a cluster of little houses and farm places. Port after stormy seas—a pure sweet dream: all is gentle, wonderfully quiet; you coast in under mainsail, absorbing the scene, the little homestead in its green meadow, the wharf, the cargo schooner at anchor, the sloop further in, a cluster of dories, and an old quaint vessel that you identify as a Quoddy sloop, a relic of another century still afloat, with stumpy mast and long boom cocked over its pinky stern.

This is Cutler, the snuggest haven in the eastern coast, or perhaps in the world. It must have been there for generations, or centuries, but to you it is a discovery, a revelation, and you anchor in the quiet water with a feeling of ultimate comfort, as though you had arrived in heaven. You go ashore to stroll, to see people and houses, perhaps to buy a half peck of new peas and a couple of small lobsters. You would say that life has nothing better to offer.

Another night, clear now, and dry, and quiet: the northwester dies away, then freshens for a while in the dawn, then gives up; the day waits for the sou'wester, the good sea breeze. A bold wild coast eastward, great cliffs, no harbors, a straight run with flood tide to East Quoddy Head. Now you can feel the great rush of the Fundy tide, a force you have to go with and constantly reckon with—and while it is with you you sweep along past the headlands as though your destiny requires it. No backtracking now. And there off to the southeast is that misty high wall of Grand Manan, the folded cliffs reaching on and on like a vast gray curtain hanging along the horizon. No life, no motion anywhere, except the dark brush of the breeze and the white breaking of surf on the shore of the main. Then East Quoddy, the candy-striped tower, the last end of the country, and beyond it to the north the opening waters of Passamaquoddy Bay, the white town of Lubec, the islands of Canada. And a fierce inward rush of tide, a river.

In the long run of life you lose the edge of adventure; you get used to strangeness; you have done it all before. Some may hold the illusion longer than others, but it seems to me that our times are against it. The only strangeness left is in space, outer and inner. But we two young cruisers were full of the innocence and poetry of our discoveries: the ugliness of Jonesport, the old melodrama, the run to Cutler, the Quoddy sloop, the vast cliffs of an uninhabited coast, the mysterious gray curtain of Grand Manan—now the new world of Lubec and Eastport, the Fundy tides, the foreign lands. And perhaps best of all the risk and pleasure of our little boat and her fast passage through the strange waters.

But much is ahead of us. The tough part of Maine cruising is going the other way, westward, to windward. You see them today going west under power, not bothering with the long beat: or they run offshore under power and then come on the port tack for a close reach to merge with the land again. In the tidal guts and bores they use power.

Our little craft is easy to handle, and fast; she can be

sculled, towed with oars, anchored, and she moves with the lightest breath. But beating against the fresh westerlies is a strain on her. First day a northwester, dark blue and silvery: a long starboard tack close-hauled, twenty miles westward with strong ebb kicking up a steep little chop and puffs and williwas striking down from the cliffs and headlands—then the rougher waters of Machias Bay, the pounding and jarring of the long-bowed hull driving into it, and then suddenly a heavy crack and jolt—something broken, a starboard shroud gone slack. The mast could have gone over—lucky she has two stays on a side. Round quick on the other tack, heave to in the fuss of choppy waters and little squalls—slack sheets and run back to a lee under Cross Island, work in toward a bight in the great cliffs, close to the steep rubbly beach where sea swells roll and break. We anchor (deep water, rock bottom), furl sail, lie rolling and pitching. One of us, my companion, more capable, goes aloft, hoisted in a sling on the jib halyard—he has pliers, extra wire, marline, and for a half hour he works while the masthead whips back and forth in the roll. He resplices the tempered wire, wraps it, binds it, says he hopes it will do—he admits to being dizzy and seasick. But the anchor comes free, we are under way again, once more fetching into the rough waters of the bay. Jonesport at last, in the quiet dusk of a long clear twilight—a fine run for a little boat, close hauled all day, pounding into it, with a broken shroud and at the last a fierce head tide. But then more pounding next day, more wind and sea, a sou'wester this time, a big one for us, perhaps twenty five or thirty knots with the tidal sea off Petit Manan too much for us. Everything wet, cabin a

shambles, water sloshing, rail under, boat almost unman-
ageable—it seems to me now that it must have been blowing forty knots, but I suppose it wasn't. I remember the
wonderful relief of a lee under Bois Bubert Island, and
anchoring and pumping out and rowing ashore and climbing a hill to look out at the smoky waters seaward to the
ghostly shaft of Petit Manan far away in the mists. It will
moderate, we said foolishly—it always does, we said, and at
five o'clock got up anchor and plunged into it again with
reefed sail. And again the slamming and crashing and the
sloshing water and the head-on fight to make to windward—and this time the bobstay fetches loose, and again
we almost lose the mast. Away now quick, sheets eased,
jib doused—bowsprit is useless, of course! We almost made
the bar—there's the channel can buoy a half mile ahead,
just visible in dusk: the great light of 'Tit Manan is flashing now; you can see it gleam on the churning waters. But
we run for it, logy with bilge water, wet, tired, released
from fright, aware of bad judgment in being there, but
heading now for shelter straight up into the still waters of
Pigeon Hill Bay. Wind easing at last, quiet night coming,
hot supper, sleep.

A quiet morning too, all restored, hopeful again, eager
for a day's ventures. Danger and folly and weariness are
trifles in a boy's day. In the dawn we borrow tools from
a moored lobster boat and fix the bowsprit and bobstay
(we are ill-equipped for such work), and once more begin
the long beat out to that sinister tower, always it seems
far on the windward horizon. But all is gentle. The early
day is muffled in mist and pale sunlight, and the sea heaves
and falls in slow undulations. We hear the steady rever-

berations of surf, like the passing of distant trains. Yesterday's wind has left a big swell, and as we slowly work out to the big outer ledges we see the breakers rearing and poising and then avalanching. But breeze is very light, sea moves lazily, we drift out to the dread bar and hang poised there waiting for a puff to give us way against the tide. Even the lighthouse seems benign, though incredibly tall: we study it with glasses, noting the trusses and struts that stiffen the stone shaft; but we see no one—in all this cruise we have been as alone as though we were invisible. The only sails we have sighted are the distant schooners, specially the huge four-master in Quoddy Roads, which got under way in the northwester as we passed and headed off shore on a starboard reach, topsails and all, doing twelve knots over the horizon.

Bass Harbor that day, back in known waters, dodging among the yachts of Mount Desert, and now a short day's run from home. All familiar and easy. The boat is leaking steadily now, everything is wet; we think home thoughts, baths, dry clothes, good cooking. We are young enough, resilient, careless, strong of body, immensely happy, but this has been a tough cruise: it is good to be only a short run from home. So—a morning easterly. A hard one, white water outside the harbor mouth, fog, rain: but home is west, straight down wind. Another folly, of course. We have sense enough to close-reef the mainsail, but once out there we are caught in what I can soberly (forty-five years after) describe as a gale. We get in the jib at once, before it blows away. We lower the peak of the small reefed main. We are swept with blown water. We charge off across the churning surface of Blue Hill

Bay, broaching in the worst squalls, but aiming for Naskeag. Our tender swamps—the air seems thick with water:
I plan to cut the tender loose, thinking it will drag under,
but it comes on with bow up and stern awash. We charge,
at times seem to plane. Seas are not big, we are in a lee of
islands, but the surface froths. Then the harbor mouth,
Naskeag, the high island, and suddenly we are in a sort of
vacuum of quiet, under a cliff to windward. We anchor.
High up in trees the wind makes a noise like jets, but down
here the water is black with stillness. We bail and pump and
wring out. I am still scared and trembling and almost
faint. We make a pot of hot soup. We sit there in a mystic
sort of silence, drinking soup, eating, repossessing our
souls and bodies. And that's about the end: the gale passes,
fog persists, we run serenely up the length of Eggemoggin
Reach on the failing southeasterly. We come home very
tired.

It is not always that way, of course. Even east of
Schoodic the winds can be light, the weather serene, but
after many years of cruising I think the fogs are thicker
down there—and certainly the tides are fiercer. A sailor,
like a woodsman, seldom admits to being lost; he knows
where he thinks he is: but at least once down there I have
lost all bearings, have been swept off into unknown waters,
have anchored to the sound of breakers unmarked anywhere on any chart. The boy in the lobster boat who towed
me into Lakeman's Harbor next day rightly marked me for
a summer sailor who had no right to mess around in his
waters. But what of the strangers with no charts, the
Champlains and Smiths, and the heavy old tubs they sailed
through all those dangerous coasts? Tides and fogs must be

the same. The soundings too are the same—at least in eastern Maine where the bottom is rock.

For deep-water cruisers there are other purposes and pleasures, but for the coastwise explorer the great thing is the scene, the freshness and beauty of islands and headlands, the channels and reaches and harbors, the forests and farms and villages. The Maine island seems to be designed to beguile the heart: it has a cove and beach for shelter on the north, a granite rampart facing open sea on the south, a meadow, a lost farm with cellar and pasture walls, a thick and tangled forest with green glades and flowers and singing thrushes, with berries and beds of crowberry moss. Every explorer has a sense of particular discovery as though the place had waited through all its centuries just for him; he feels attached to it by ties that are almost mystic, he seems to have known about it before, and he ventures into its inner places with a premonition of discovery as though he might be walking in a recurring dream: here is the old meadow, the filled-in well, the stones—here are the glades, the big spruces. The boom of surf comes from seaward—there's a sea-facing beach of round stones, a deep cove like a kettle, and a century-old pile of driftwood, all waiting for him to see them and find them.

And the harbors, the quiet havens hidden from a noisy world—you spend your life going back to them, searching for them. Cutler, Lakeman's, Roque, Cape Split, Bunker's —in a way there is no end to them: Burnt Coat, Webb's, Swayne's, Buck's, Pulpit, Duck. . . . After a lifetime of searching you still find one somewhere, perhaps you are directed to it by a recognizable act of fate—as I was once led into Little River near the mouth of the Damariscotta in thick fog and dusk, weaving through breaking ledges and anchoring in the still pond inside. They are haunted by old ghosts, those harbors: you remember Joshua Slocum bringing the *Spray* to anchor in Round Pond, and Captain Argyll charging into Somes Sound bent on violence, and the pirates and sixteenth century fishermen lurking about Monhegan and putting into Damariscove for water, and the old settlers of Richmond Island, and the Plymouth men trading for furs up the rivers. You sail up the broad sound of the St. George's River and remember that Captain Weymouth reported that it would shelter great fleets and navies—and perhaps you note the snug little anchorage of Pleasant Point Gut where the immortal sloop-builder Wilbur Morse was born. And that oldest of the known harbors on the coast, called New Harbor, too crowded now for the quiet cruiser. And the ancient sea battles, off Pemaquid and Castine and Small's Cove on Deer Isle, where a few iron cannon balls may still be seen. And life itself, going on by sea and shore for four centuries.

There may be other coasts. My travels have mostly been in New England. The Aegean has been called the true realm of gold, but to a sailor of small boats it seems forbidding with its barren heights and depths. In Maine we have what are affectionately called eel ruts and gunk holes, and those with all the rest, even including the fog, make it the cruiser's true home.

ELEVEN

FOG

The fog, which till this moment had held off,
now lowered over the sea like a pall. I was in a
world of fog, shut off from the universe. . . . It
continued so for a number of days, the wind
increasing to a gale. The waves rose high, but I had
a good ship. Still, in the dismal fog I felt myself
drifting into loneliness, an insect on a straw in the
midst of the elements.

Joshua Slocum

FOG ALONG THE COAST of Maine makes a fourth or
fifth dimension. It comes from the cold off-shore
waters. It masses and waits for the change of wind,
the southeast slant that pushes it into bays and reaches.
"Wind's out," they say, with a twist of chin to mark the
finality of it. "She's out," they say. Out of the southwest,
into the southeast. That's about all they say. "Out"—out
to the eastward somewhere, to that blank moonlike world
of solid mist with no bearings and no visible dimensions.
If you are in it, caught in it, you move with faith and fear,
one eye on the only mark left, your compass, the other on
the third wave-crest ahead, which is as far as you can see.
If you are running with a motor, you can't hear. If you
don't know your speed you can't reckon your distance.
Unseen tides carry you. Great rolling ground-swells slip

under you, heaving you high and low, looming and vanishing, and in your mind you see them rearing and cresting, the black ledges underneath, the avalanche of white water, the boat rolled and crushed like a toy. . . .

It comes in many guises. There is the shining fog of a summer morning, too bright for the eyes, with blue above and silky windless water below, and your heart is full of hope for a fine day, with southwest wind and clear horizons: but take warning—that white and sunny innocence out there can be as opaque as wool; a cloud in the sun, a point or two shift of breeze, and it can last out the day. But if the sun prevails and the summer breeze holds west of south, all is well and the solid coast and the ledges and cliffs and forests emerge in ceramic brightness. The fog is seen to be beautiful and theatrical and makes silvery streamers in the golden sunlight and then vanishes forever. In the noontime of a clear and classic summer day it seems as unlikely and improbable as a night's dream.

There is the cold, iron-gray fog that comes in with an easterly and means business. It looks like doom. It is opaque and relentless. It carries the feel of icebergs and arctic wastes. It moves in steadily, with deadly intent—you see it coming at you like a massed attack, and when it strikes it does it with a rush and a sudden cold darkness and wetness, and you know at once that you are in for it. If you are ashore and secure you none the less tremble a little, you feel the menace of it, the old northern dangers, the memory of wrecks and lost ships; and if you are out in it you summon up all your resources and tune yourself up to the highest pitch of alertness and cunning. Even in a small craft you know you are risking everything. With five or

six feet of draught under you, several tons of boat and
ballast, you hold your breath listening and watching, you
almost hear the clang of a distant bell or the moan of a
buoy, you see shadowy visions in the opaque air—cliffs,
headlands, rearing breakers, you almost feel the surge of
undertow, the beginnings of catastrophe, the crunching and
rending of timbers. . . .

But no doubt you are brave. You are captain and
navigator and crew. The course is surely right, east a half
north; the old compass is steady and trustworthy; the chart
shows deep water here and a bell there off the ledges—the
chart is perfectly logical and clear, like geometry, and
transforms the whole invisible coast with its breakers and
shoals into a simple proposition of degrees and soundings
and nautical miles. And you are here on a pleasure trip,
you are vacationer, idler, playing at a way of life, inviting
danger and death for the fun of it. Somewhere inshore of
you, among more dangerous ledges, is a lobsterman working for his living—you can just hear the mutter of his
engine as he circles his traps. He is real, you think; he
counts, he knows his business, he slips among the breakers
with easy confidence, he goes safely home to harbor, he
sells his lobsters. Is that more like life than this? More
necessary? You think it is, you respect him, your spirit is
strengthened by the thought of him, and the sound of his
distant motor, but meanwhile the long rollers come heaving out of the white wall a boat's length away. The wet
wind blows steady from south-southeast, water drips from
all the rigging, the sloop reaches along with quiet speed,
east a half north, seconds and minutes tick off, surf sounds
faintly, faintly—you feel it in your blood, you strain to

hear the first clang of the bell, you watch and watch and watch till all your senses are merged in the gray rolling sea and the swirling fog.

But if the bell is never heard, what then? The calculation is wrong, the compass for once betrays, or some unseen tidal current, and you miss your bell, your landfall —you are suddenly in unknown waters, beyond all reckonings. The chart is no good any more—these ledges you hear snarling to windward are surely unmarked and unheard of—and is that a loom of land ahead, a great headland unrecorded on any chart? or is it a black ledge quite close, right under the bow? or is it anything at all? The coast—the main, as they say there—must be to the north; it always has been. Open sea to the south. Those are the realities. But in between, where we are now, nothing but unknown danger. The bell is gone, the bearings are gone, we may be here or there—if we keep on we'll be somewhere in that vast and perilous confusion of sunken shoals where the waters seethe and break at all tides in all weathers. Perhaps then in a moment of preternatural silence comes one faint *clang*, far away, off the port quarter it seems. Another half minute and we'd have missed it forever. But bear away quick, coast down wind, quiet as quiet, listening—compass northwest now—listening, hearing nothing, not a solitary sound, no bird cry, no splash, only perhaps the rustle of the tender towing behind, and *there*—there's the thing itself, a dim triangle on the water, half mist, off the port beam, not a sound from it—you wonder if it is real, is there at all, if it isn't your dream. What ails it? What's a bell buoy for? And then you hear it clanging and banging away, the loud ugly clash of iron on iron. The sound crashes against your ears.

But you know fog is like that. You know bell buoys are like that. You remember all the near misses, the close shaves of the past, the freakish chances of sound and sight—you remember coming close up on Whitehead and seeing the jet of white steam shoot out of the whistle at fifteen second intervals, and you didn't hear a sound of it; and you remember too hearing that same whistle on quiet nights twenty miles away. But now you are on your course again, east by north a quarter north, you know where you are, the chart is clear and obvious in your mind's eye, that *terra incognita* of desperate seas and half-tide ledges has receded, is lurking elsewhere. Some day you'll be in it, you'll be lost and gone—you know it can happen, you remember that classic mariner Captain Slocum in the gales and fogs of Cape Horn, coping with the most desperate navigational crises ever faced by a lone sailor, and you shrug off your little uncertainties. You are back on your track again, watching and listening for the next mark.

My own failings as a navigator are partly due to a too easy trust in luck. The box compass came into the family sixty years ago, is a sort of heirloom, has never been adjusted, is a bit slow to respond. Other equipment is even less suitable. No protractors, direction finders, depth finders—no current tables or formulae for calculating tidal set, no pelorus, no patent log or speed gauge. Courses plotted by means of a small rectangular hatch cover, manipulated over the chart on the cockpit floor. But the whole business is anachronistic anyway, a deliberate folly, a playful reversion to Columbus or John Smith. You cope with what you think of as basic nature, wind and water, breaking shoals and fog. You see what you can do on your own, unaided, with only sail and oar for power. You have a little contempt for the man who installs a fortune's worth of equipment to insure himself against the dangers of the sea. You remember old Slocum sailing round the world with a tin alarm clock to navigate by, and cotton sails, hemp rope, solid spars, and no power.

Take a mind's eye view of Casco Bay on a summer morning. Wind southerly, about twelve knots—and by "southerly" I mean it has the look and feel of a south-wester but is coming from the point of due south. *Festina* is reaching from the Mark Island beacon off Harpswell about east by south for the Small Point bell. No course plotted, no compass uncovered, wind abeam, sea blue and sun out, horizons hazy, white fingers of cirrus high in the seaward sky—a fine sailing morning, with the sloop streaking along at an easy six knots, slanting up and over the long roll making in from the south. Air chill and palpably damp, even in the sun. Land to the north seems dim and far, part of a shoreward world of its own. I hold the tiller with almost a caress, thinking how sweetly and quietly she runs, with no fuss forward and no ripple aft; I am half hypnotized by the motion and the dazzle and the steady rustle and seethe of the waters. My wife lies on the lee seat, drowsy under a big sun hat. And then suddenly the breeze gives out, stops, seems to be turned off; the main-sail flaps, the boat rolls. A cold feel of new air from ahead —I see a thread of wool yarn on the starboard shroud fling itself out, then drop. The old breeze comes back, the southerly—we heel a little, steady down on course again, surge along, then hesitate, flap, roll to windward. No southerly breeze any more, and a strange coldness in the air—and there looming in from the southeast is a great wall of fog, a mile off, a half mile, shining like a range of snow with puffs and streamers of gold on its sunny crests.

A new breeze now. Southeast, gentle but with the feel of icebergs. She's "out," as they say. Quickly the compass, bearings on Ragged Island, the White Bull Ledge: the bell off Small Point is already gone. Sheets in now, close hauled, rail dipping—for a few minutes the northward lands show clear, still in golden sunlight, then the whiteness surges over. It is cold and relentless and strangely dark; it is a substance, a wetness, a close wall round us.

So in an instant all is changed. We are blind, bereft of comfort and safety, lost in a deathlike dimension of whiteness. Nothing of the world exists but a circle of heaving gray water. It is always the same, without mark or feature, yet it moves, it looms on one side and swings us up to a silent crest and slides away, up and away. No sound except the faint seethe and rustle of the boat as she reaches ahead into the white wall.

Now the bell is to windward. We can't fetch it. East by north is the best we can do with sheets trimmed in close. I remember the bearing on the ledge called the White Bull—a quick guess before it vanished—and line up my hatch cover on the compass on the chart. I make a penciled cross lightly. I admire the clarity of the chart; I see the little cross as a reassurance: there we *are* in a fine blank area of deep water. All must so far be well, though this is surely the thickest fog ever seen. No fog on the chart, though. There lies Cape Small with its two off-lying ledges, one with a spindle, the other with a beacon and flashing light—but of course we can't fetch it on this tack. East by north takes us in against the main shore, just outside a red nun buoy and a cluster of dangerous rocks. Do we tack and keep outside of everything, or do we hold on for the shore of Cape Small trusting to see the loom of it before we hit it, hoping to be on the right side of the red nun? Tide ebbing. *Festina* goes where she points. We hold on. Tide should set us to windward. Two miles or so—are we doing five knots? Probably less. That's about twenty-five minutes. With this big roll coming in there'll be surf; we are already listening for it.

What do you see first? The white of breakers? The high loom of trees? Deadly brown kelp under the bow? You focus your senses until they seem useless; your eyes are shocked by the shadowy crest of a roller or a floating gull that suddenly looks as big as a vessel. The whiteness ahead is surely darkening, is turning into silhouettes—but then it isn't. You hear the rumble of surf, or is it the roaring of your ears and blood? The nun buoy is like a wraith in your sight—you are well to windward of it but perhaps that's it after all—surely something is off there on your port beam.

Then it is *there*, right ahead, a thing, black, white—a rock awash, a wave breaking and thundering. Tiller is down, sails flap, blocks rattle. Cape Small itself? Cape Horn, it looked like. A glimpse of doom. No landmark, nothing but dangerous rock and dangerous sea. But now on the port tack, heading off shore, we are alone again in the circle of rolling water. The chart is there, damp now on the cockpit floor, but plain and certain; and here *we* are, more or less, or at least I hope we are: the red nun and the shoals are behind us—they must be, but I stare into the white, forward and both sides. You never know. Compass steady at south-southwest now, but it might have had a spasm—did I put a jackknife beside it, or a monkey wrench?

Here we go, anyway, round again on the starboard tack, heading in once again for that unknown coast, watching, listening, the same as before. Is it still there? Deep shores, as the chart guarantees? Again the sudden blow of black rock and white foam against the eyes, and this time I hold it in view, I see a great timber lodged at high-water mark; I see grass, trees, a headland further on—it is the real world after all, *terra firma* itself. But the sea is building up in bigger ranges as it rushes in, I can feel the scend of it as the boat rolls high and low. We tack again into deep water, we work outward to clear the point. We never hear or see the bell buoy, or the outer ledge with the spindle, but we tack again, we slip past Small Point itself—we see the dark rocks of it clearly as the fog lifts a little over the warmer land; we get a ghostly glimpse of the other off-lying ledge with its white beacon above the foam of breaking sea.

Then all is gone, swallowed in the gray silence. We are alone in our tiny circle of reality. Close-hauled still, starboard tack, just able to hold a course for one of the Seguin passages four nautical miles away. Watch for lobster buoys to see how tide is running—the currents do unexpected things in these waters. No buoys, though—nothing visible, no way of seeing the tidal flow. I assume it will set us to windward still, and remember the grim warnings in the old *Coast Pilot* about dangerous waters off the mouth of the Kennebec—where we are now. Tides, winds, and reefs can be ferocious, they say. There have been famous and splendid disasters. But now, out here in open water, all is lonesome and quiet. I sink into a kind of hypnotic revery, watching compass and luff of sail and the wall of whiteness beyond the bow. No sound—not even from the great diaphone horn on Seguin that sometimes on still nights reverberates along the whole coast. No mutter of boat engines anywhere, though on good summer days processions pass across these waters. Perhaps another noise-less sailing craft somewhere? You have to keep watching, but you have the notion that yours is the only cruising craft on the coast with no motor.

Seguin Island is a rocky mountain rising from the sea off the mouth of the Kennebec River, and there are four ways of getting past it. In fog the sensible way is to go well outside with deep water and no reefs and a whistling buoy to turn on. But the course out there to the buoy is south-east, almost dead to windward. Or I could ease sheets a bit and follow the coast line across the mouth of the Kenne-bec, but then in Sheepscot Bay I'd be too far to leeward—and on the way I'd have to contend with those celebrated tides and shoals I'm fearful of. A picture flashes in my mind of the old Fort Popham settlers in 1607 contending with these same tides and shoals, and this same fog. No charts, no buoys, no bells and diaphones. A legend, I think, almost too remote and strange to believe. It is one of the worst spots on the New England coast. I still watch the luff, the compass, the fog wall, but for a few moments my mind is full of those tough and competent men—I see them conning their tublike little ships out through the channels, a man at the masthead to warn of reefs, to watch for fog: how could they tack, I wonder—how could they beat out against the everlasting southerly winds and the rushing tides?

There, reverberating from far, far away, the great horn of Seguin. Too far to hear or place—it comes like something remembered.

We are on one of the two middle passages, heading for the channel between the northern end of Seguin and Ellingwood Rock. Almost due compass east. Sheets eased about four inches. The breeze is gentle but perfectly steady as though it had settled down to a serious day-long operation and *Festina* slips along with no sound except the little surge under her lee bow. The sails are as motionless as molded metal. The long swells heave and roll out of the fog but the boat seems to be fixed to its own track and speeds along with mysterious power.

The sound of the diaphone comes louder, then recedes, then fades away. It fills the air but has no source. I watch the time, listen for boats, for surf, stare into the white, shake myself out of the trancelike monotony, wipe the water from eyes and face, wait for a sign, a loom, a break. An hour—surely no more, more likely fifty minutes. My wife is snoozing in a lee bunk below. I'm alone outside, and cold and rather wet, and my hands have a strange corpselike consistency as though they were made of slightly melted wax, but I am too preoccupied to bother with such things. My senses are as alert as I can make them; I watch and listen, watch and listen, with steady tension.

This time it is the dark loom of cliff, the high north-west face of Seguin Island making a little lee under the

fog. I see the passage now, I see Ellingwood Rock to port
—an easy landfall for once; I bear away to keep clear of the
windless pocket under the high island, and I see the cliffs
dissolving upward into the white. My navigation is seldom
as good as this, and I have a sense of victory—or perhaps
luck. Now bear away a point and a half to pass between
Tom's Rock and the ledges called The Sisters, then hold
straight on across the mouth of Sheepscot Bay for the
bell buoy off The Cuckolds.

So—hours of silence and blindness. The waves break on
The Sisters to port, the pyramid of timbers takes shadowy
shape for a few seconds, then vanishes. Nothing for a long
time, except the distant thud of a heavy motor heading
seaward to pass the whistler outside Seguin. No horns, no
other boats, but the breeze holds as steady as fate. Wetness
fills the air, rigging drips, spars are beaded with water.
Then from somewhere ahead a new reverberation, higher
pitched than Seguin—and again, stronger, off the port
bow. The Cuckolds Light, on a ledge among breaking
ledges. Good horn, just where it should be. But no sound of
a bell yet, nor do I really expect it, though I strain to listen.
Nothing else changes.

Then suddenly—something ahead, white, a hull, a boat
lifting on a sea. Out with foghorn, quick. But then a bell,
loud and close, and the boat heaves full in view, a big motor
boat, and people, and the bell buoy there too, harshly
clanging. A fishing party, using the bell as an anchor—
illegally, of course, but hidden from all eyes but mine. They
line the rails with rods and lines, and *Festina* brushes past as
silent as a phantom—I don't think they see her at all; they
aren't watching anything but their fish lines. In a moment

I see the cliffs dissolving upward into the white

we are gone and alone again in the circle of fog.

A long day, it seems. We could slip into Boothbay Harbor, a busy and noisy anchorage, but we are going well, we seem to be on a sort of track. Same breeze, same course, same good luck, and maybe we can make Christmas Cove. I see it there on the chart, the perfect haven; I check off the courses, the buoys, Ram Island Light with its bell, the beacon right at the mouth of the cove, all clear and easy on the chart. Tide will be flooding up the Damariscotta River, the breeze in there should be on our starboard beam—all very good. And the snug cove waiting, a spare mooring to pick up, and the perfect stillness of a foggy night.

We hold on for another hour. The air begins to darken, the breeze is lighter; I think of night coming, of blackness and fog together, and my whole being yearns for that safe cove still far ahead. Then abruptly right above us, it seems, a deep bronze BOOM, at first a terror shooting down to the base of my spine, then instantly a joy, a release: the big bell of Ram Island, all serene and confident, reverberating in the vast fog stillnesses. No wave noises here: we are in the lee of islands, and the bell booms out thrillingly. All is well, another course made good, and we slip past the bell and the light, leaving them to starboard, not seeing them —fog if anything is thicker in the failing breeze.

But now we are fetching in against the shore of the main, at Ocean Point; the breeze heads us and we have to tack at last to get round Green Island. At the slatting of sails and shift of angle my wife comes out and stands in the companionway and peers round. She sees nothing. We hear the surf on Green Island—the old roll of the sea is coming in on us from the southeast again. We come round on the starboard tack again—one more mark to reach, a black can buoy, and then the last leg to the mouth of Christmas Cove.

But our destiny is otherwise. Over-confidence, perhaps—that and an outdated chart. All the way from Casco Bay without missing a mark, a serene and easy passage through the tides and shoals of the Kennebec—and now suddenly failure, confusion, near disaster. In "The Wreck of the *Hesperus*" the skipper is made to laugh a scornful laugh, but I never knew a veteran seaman who was scornful of the hazards of the sea; he is in truth more often nervous and cautious. Nothing is sure until it is over and done with: at least that is the moral of this story. Nothing is ever sure in a fog.

We are heading for a black can buoy near the mouth of the Damariscotta River; there we shall turn more northward and run straight for the entrance of Christmas Cove, passing close to the northern end of Heron Island. It is the simplest navigational problem of the day; all I am concerned about is the tidal current that will suck us up the river. I look at the chart again, the trustworthy reality that has brought me through the unseen mysteries of fog. All is now clear.

Then suddenly a familiar old sound, a clanging bell buoy. It is off to port, at first unseen, then as I swing toward it it materializes. a solid black-and-white pyramid tilting slowly back and forth on the smooth swells. Undoubtedly an authentic regulation buoy. It is not on my chart. Ordinarily nothing is more reassuring than a black and white bell, but now I am caught by surprise, I think quickly and inaccurately. They have set it in the main channel of the

river, I decide; black and white bells are set in the middle
of channels—that's what they are for. It must be outside the
black can—bells are usually well out in deep water. I must
use it to turn on, I suppose. I'm farther out than I expected
—some tidal current must be pushing us out. I must swing
more northerly.

All this reasoning is wrong, of course. But mind works
with the speed of light, and in an instant I am on a new
course, heading for Christmas Cove, as I think.

The heave of a swell about to break is a movement of
grandeur; you watch it gather and mount in a slow cre-
scendo, up and up, easy and lazy and vast—you watch for
the opening white crest, then the curl of it, the dark green
like liquid glass advancing, rushing, crashing, crashing in a
huge shatter of foam. It is what happens now right ahead of
Festina, right there beyond her bow. She comes round on a
pivot, gathers way again, moves slowly away from the
breaking water. Back to the sound of the bell, to the sight
of it rocking sluggishly. Another course, this time figured
carefully. The bell must be out there in deep water, it
must be. So the mind insists. But then—more breakers.
The mind fails, it whirls and gropes. The rocks are all
round; I can hear the roar and crunch of falling water; I
am lost in an unknown sea, on an unseen coast. The clear
and logical chart has no relevance to all this and the
anonymous bell buoy begins to seem like a sinister decoy
arranged by some regional demon. Yet I hold to it as the
last hope, I keep it in view, or in hearing, as we grope for
a way out. It is only later, next day, that I realize that I
should have kept faithfully to my original course, passed
outside it, picked up the black can—it is only a quarter of a

mile or so beyond, exactly as the chart shows.

But now, groping and all but lost forever, I see a low rift in the white, a dark edge of shore, and something that might be a boat—not far, quite close, in fact: a boat moored, a quiet spot, a shelter. Dusk is falling, breeze fades to almost nothing, the roar of breakers seems louder all round, but now quickly I see where we are, I have a revelation: a harbor is there beyond, a haven called Little River, as narrow as a bottle, ringed with ledges—even on the chart it looks unapproachable, and here in fog and dusk it is surely impossible. But we are in the mouth, we slip past the moored boat, we could toss a stone into the trees to port—then a house, a small wharf, more boats, fishing boats, lobster traps, no yachts, a deep still pond, and we come sliding in as silently as a shadow and round up in a slow U turn and drift to a stop. Perfect stillness everywhere—water as motionless as black paint. Anchor down in twenty feet, sails loosely furled, lines coiled and set for the night, tender snugged in, mosquito nets rigged—no riding light here, nothing will move on this water till dawn. I listen for a minute to the reverberation from the ledges outside, the sounds of doom and catastrophe far off now, a continuum that fills the night with elemental splendor.

I hear the stove going below, I smell soup, feel warmth. I crawl in—the cabin is a small one—and take off wet garments and sink back among pillows with as much comfort as the son of old Odysseus took among Nestor's handmaidens. It is luck, of course, undeserved and miraculous, but I accept it as one of the inscrutable mysteries of the fog.

TWELVE

ALONG SHORE

You shall scarce finde any Baye, shallow
shore, or Cove of sand, where you may not take many
Clampes, or Lobsters, or both at your pleasure; and
in many places lode your boat as you please: nor Iles
where you finde not fruits, birds, crabs, and muskles,
or all of them, for the taking at a lowe water.

Captain John Smith

OWNING A BOAT gives one pride and pleasure and the
illusion of far horizons. The moment you float in
your own craft you share the same destiny as the
old adventurers; you pass beyond the shelter of the cove and
set a course for Gull Ledge shimmering in the sunlight a
quarter of a mile off shore. You reckon with the elemental
dangers of tides and winds and fogs; you take on the heavy
responsibilities of master and owner, and give commands.
The safety of wife, child, and friend is in your hands. Your
eyes narrow against the dazzle of sea and sky; your expres-
sion assumes the inscrutable look of authority, you study
the signs and portents; you alone perceive the loom of the
Wandering Rocks, and the shadow of Scylla to port and
Charybdis to starboard.

The sea, like the top of Everest, is there. Beyond Gull
Ledge is Goose Rock, beyond Goose Rock the Porcupines
bristle against the edge of the sky. Headlands and capes

dwindle away into infinity. What you need is a larger boat —a sea-keeping boat. You could voyage some day to Isle au Haut, perhaps to Matinicus, or beyond into the unknown Ocean Stream. You remember a classmate named Martindale, a quiet chap, steady and self-contained and a bit shy —when last heard of he was heading westward through the Solomon Islands, single-handed in a thirty-foot yawl. The idea fills you with yearnings. After all, he was no prodigy; he was just a nice guy whose family ran a furnace and plumbing business in Brockton.

So you are caught in a dream of boats. You get a boat. You marry her. In time perhaps you quarrel; you lose all patience with her failings—she leaks, is always wet, is slow, too small, too fat; you discard her (with emotions of guilt) and at once you get another. You are hooked. You can't live without a boat. But from the beginning of this affair you never reckoned with the complications and compulsions. For a poor and modest man any sort of boat can be both expensive and burdensome. Keeping a live mistress would probably be simpler.

In older days it could all be done more naturally—the haulings and launchings and the repairing and caulking and painting and rigging, and the moorings and landing floats and outhauls and tenders. Every cove had men of ability who could do anything for two dollars a day wages. It hardly occurs to a new owner of a keel sloop that his little vessel, weighing three or four tons, drawing four and a half feet, must be floated into a specially built cradle (made of solidly bolted timber), and dragged inch by inch for fifty yards up a steep shore, then either covered with a weather-proof roof of some sort or hauled into a specially

All along shore

built house. The mast—thirty-five feet or more—must be hoisted out with a derrick. All the equipment must be stored. The motor, if any, must be taken care of. Then the moorings must be brought in, the small boats stored, with the ropes, buoys, chains, shackles, anchors, rollers, blocks, tackles, crowbars, pries, jacks, timbers—plus the indescribable junk that is essential to a boat-yard operation. And of course at the start of another season all must be done in reverse, with the addition of scraping, sanding, caulking, puttying, painting and varnishing, together with repair and renewal of all gear and the acquisition of new and expensive equipment.

The modern owner avoids some of these involvements in two ways. He buys only the new synthetic equipment, the glass-fibered boat, the gear impervious to rust and rot, or he turns the whole problem over to a yacht-yard and pays the bills. The annual cost may seem to him as great as the basic worth of his boat, but by this time he is in no position to be cautious. He is committed. What his boat demands, she gets.

Synthetic material does simplify maintenance work, but none the less a sea-going sailing craft is still a deep, heavy body and a complicated structure of spars and wires. And somehow modern needs lead us into complication: we have a motor to take care of, an electrical system, refrigeration, a gas stove, hot and cold running water, a depth finder, direction finder. . . .

In earlier times, the whole affair seemed a basic part of the coast life. You began by cutting down trees. You needed rollers and pries and poles and timber for the cradle, two long girders for the base, four cross members for the keel to rest on, all bolted with inch- thick galvanized bolts countersunk in the bottom of the girders. You set up at least four posts to support the bilges, braced, angled, and measured carefully: a post two inches too long might crush the planking as though it were an eggshell. With luck you might find some sound timbers along the beaches, even good, milled four-by-sixes or four-by-fours. You needed crow bar, ax, saw, augur, heavy hammer, wrench, bolts, galvanized nails.

In due time you pried and skidded your finished cradle down to a point on the low-tide shore where you guessed your vessel would float in safely—and woe to you if she didn't: she might be stuck half in and half out, no more moving. You had to pile stones on the cradle, of course, to keep it on the bottom—and it was well to fasten a line to it just in case the stones got knocked off by unexpected turmoil of sea. (I lost a cradle that way once—it simply vanished into wind and water and was never seen again.)

At this point, with cradle ready and empty, you had to make several decisions. If you were using rollers, did you set them in place under the waiting cradle or did you bring your boat in first and then slip them under her? And if you did that, how did you lift the whole structure? One of the essential tools was a spruce tree about fifteen-feet long and six-inches thick at the base, a pry that needed a Paul Bunyan to wield it properly. But of course lifting a four-ton mass, even one corner of it, is to be avoided if possible; better to get the tracks and rollers in place first. But rollers themselves are unbelievably cussed. I used them for years: the long ones are bad enough, short ones are worse. They twist, jam, stick, refuse to budge, and then roll giddily backward. Better drag her on greased planks—I say that after years of stubborn struggle with rollers.

But what have you done about the mast? Mine was forty feet from truck to step, and weighed with all its rigging well over three-hundred pounds. A wharf and derrick do the job easily, but what if you have nothing but a rocky shore? You rig shear poles, with tackles and guys leading in all directions; you call upon wife, children, neighbors, and friends. You organize a mast-lifting and mast-moving campaign. In former times, of course, you had neighbors who knew exactly what to do about masts, but they are old men now.

And what power do you use for the big hauling? You can visit a quarry town and look for a second-hand winch, a slow but sure mechanism; but it must be anchored immovably, either in a concrete base or between two strong trees. You can hire a tractor, or a truck, or you can try using your own car—provided there is good ground to maneuver on. A horse or team of horses used to do well, if they were trained to it and familiar with the work of hauling and launching boats. In the far past the best available power was a team of oxen, and nothing has ever surpassed them in doing the work they were designed to do. They could work anywhere, under any conditions. They moved their bulk with ease and precision and what seemed like limitless power. They never lunged and stamped about like horses, but leaned gently ahead with exactly the right force to do what had to be done; they operated as though they were an extension of the mind of their master, moving an inch one way or another at the murmur of command, stopping on an instant, or applying more and more of their strength and weight until the task was accomplished. A good driver seemed to commune with his oxen in quiet melodies, as though he were crooning to them.

But we must settle for a tractor today, a convulsive and explosive device, but capable of all such tasks. They move mountains as well as ships.

A tackle, of course, too: pronounced *tayckle*. Two big double blocks and at least two-hundred feet of three-quarter inch manilla—but of course manilla is a vanishing substance: half-inch nylon will do the work as well, or better, at a higher price. You will need other lines and gear, perhaps a wire or chain bridle for the cradle, perhaps even a watch tackle on the main tackle. You will need a strong tree or post to anchor the upper end of the tackle. . . .

And when she is up there, safe and level on *terra firma*, you must house her, cover her, keep out the sun and rain and snow. You buy lumber, build a frame. You buy a tarpaulin. You bundle her up, knowing how the winds will rip and tear and the snows will heap up. You are filled with anxiety for her. Vandals may attack her. Squirrels may run in and out and make nests—or wasps, or mice. She will be undefended in the long stormy months. Tidal waves, cyclones, convulsions of nature—you imagine them all.

And that mast—where do you put it? From a far corner of the living room to a far corner of the kitchen? If slipped in through a window it may just fit.

I make too much of all this, though in fact I have understated my own ventures in the care and support of boats. I remember one night in early September when I had been delayed by stormy weather and thwarted by neap tides, and the one chance left to do the hauling job was

between midnight and dawn. And many a launching day
has begun all calm and serene, and you take the perfect
time to move her down to the low-tide shore—she, your
little vessel, all shining in new paint—and you wait for the
rising tide, five or six hours. But who can tell what winds
will blow? Suppose a northwest squall breaks across the
bay, as it often does on a June day; or an afternoon sou'-
wester whistling in from seaward. . . . Can you get her off
without gouges and bumps? Have you rigged lines, anchors,
a good mooring? And when and how do you get the mast
back into her?

As for moorings, they require labor and knowledge and
ingenuity. It used to be that you began with a stone, granite
or igneous, of reliable grain, a practical shape and size—say
eight- or ten-hundred pounds. You acquired two or three
drills and a sledge hammer and started to pound. You
pounded pretty steadily for several days, with frequent
visits to a blacksmith to resharpen drills. When at last you
broke through, with a feeling as of coming out at the other
side of the earth, you pried and propped your stone on
its side, inserted a forged eyebolt in the hole, built a fire
to heat the end of it, and pounded it over.

In a time like ours, dedicated wholly to avoiding hard
labor of any sort, all such operations may seem too quaint
to believe in. But they were in fact the common practices.
I remember watching George Dodge swinging a two-
handed sledge against a drill held by the bare hands of a
boy who seemed to me to be in danger of his life at every
stroke.

With a ten-foot range of tide, great lifting power is
at hand, but even so the management of mooring stones

with their chains, shackles, buoys, and other gear is a problem in engineering. You can sling a half-ton stone under a dory—in theory, at least. But if you try it in practise you fall foul of more variables and complications than you can predict. Better to use two dories, or skiffs of any sort, with a girder across: and when you bring your mooring in from deep water that's what you have to do. But it will take you two days, if not three. In theory, again, you can lift ten feet in one tide; in actuality, what with stretching, slipping, sinking, you get about six feet—and if your mooring depth at low water is eighteen feet, you'll need three lifts. Unless you work at night, that means three days. And there's always weather to contend with, or those half-hearted tides that give you less lift than you count on.

With your two boats for lifting you'll need a third to act as tender and utility boat, and you'll need an extra anchor and lines—and in the end all these items, boats, anchors, lines, timbers, chains, will have to be taken care of and stored. Your mooring apparatus will be a mass of weeds and barnacles. And you'll have a lot of other gear and an outhaul with its own mooring and perhaps a float or heavy ladder to be hauled out.

It is not necessary in these times, of course, to pound a hole by hand through a granite stone. You can buy a mushroom anchor—a two-hundred pounder, say. And if you can pay the bills, it is much simpler to turn over most of your problems to a boatyard. They have work boats and lighters and all needed apparatus. They are specialists.

But a few years ago everyone who lived in sight of the salt water was a specialist. Beginning with the standing trees in his woodlot he could build and launch and rig a vessel and sail her to the Grand Banks. In any problem concerning boats, large or small, in or out of the water, he was as expert as a trained physician. Some have kept those skills, but there is less need for them. Tasks can be done more easily with power, and things come in factory-fresh packages. The latest sailing craft in this Maine bay is a cruising yawl made of glass and shipped complete from Ohio on a trailertruck.

Changes in materials and methods are usually good in themselves, in spite of doubt and even resentment. Wood does rot and fail—so do cotton canvas and hemp rope. Bulldozers do greater deeds than oxen. Power is triumphant. To take a stand with old ways is irrational and sentimental. But loss is real too, and what is lost is the purpose and function of a people who once knew clearly what they had to do. They made use of everything at hand, the wind and the water, the seasons, the weather, the shore and rocks, the earth, the trees, the crops, the beasts. The center of their universe was right where they were, in a physical and actual sense. With their own hands and tools they made a living. They worked to live and lived to work without much concern for the political or economic crises in the world at large.

The common craft along shore is now the outboard, and boys crave them as inland boys crave hot-rod cars. An old wooden punt with a thirty-horse motor on its stern will plane on smooth water at twenty knots; she is no good in a chop. All sorts of local boats are devised for power and speed in the coves and sheltered waters, and boys use up time and fuel showing off, competing, stunting, annoying everyone in hearing distance. But the summer folk bring in fancier craft on trailers, the fiberglass models produced annually like automobiles, with accessories, and these are the longshore boats of the future. The local fishing boats will be shipped out from some inland Detroit and sold and serviced by organized dealers. Speed and power and efficiency will all increase and miracles of ingenuity will be achieved. All boating activity will be contingent on the industrial technology of the nation.

The old longshore life, like all other life, was a game, a contest for survival and comfort, but it involved less guilt and more acceptance than the newer ways of life. Respect and self-satisfaction rested mainly on a house, a barn, and a boat. Any sort of victory required skill and hard work, and perhaps moral conviction, and thanks to the puritan traditions those habits strongly endured. But the essential pattern was one of self-containment. All food and materials were at hand, in the earth, or sea, and a man's major task was to know how to use them. That was his career.

Such a man was very often conscious of the pleasure and even romance of his life. He grew up as a boy in a dream of boats. He watched the vessels come and go, and the shipwrights and riggers at work, and the sail lofts, and the life of the wharves. When he had his own sloop-boat he kept her slick and fast, and sailed her in the summer races. He talked and listened to talk in the stores and boatyards. He whittled out models. He built a skiff for duck shooting in the fall—for gunning, as he called it. He observed all the wildlife, and went out after deer sometimes, and carried on a year-round campaign against the foxes. But he took pleasure in his world: he watched the ospreys and the bald eagles and the flocks of sea ducks and families of loons. He went off with his boys in a punt to catch flounders, or to dig clams on the flats at low water—and if they needed a bit of cash they could always get twenty-five cents a bushel for the clams. And out by Channel Rock there was good handling for cod and haddock, and sometimes a big old halibut. But nothing was more pleasant than a run of mackerel in the bay, with a crowd out there in punts and skiffs and anything that would float, pulling in tinker mackerel as fast as they could get the jigs out—it was a kind of festival.

A launching was also a festival. The big vessels were dressed in flags and a band played and schools declared a holiday—such events are recorded in history. But any man getting his sloop into the water in spring counted on his neighbors as well as a collection of experts and humorists to act as chorus. If an illicit jug were available, so much the better, but the event was generally good-natured enough without benefit of whisky. Nothing seems more appropriate to life and the future than the launching of a boat. She is painted, furbished, renewed from stem to stern; she goes forth once again to encounter the dangers of wind and water; she is wholly brave and gallant; she is an emblem of hope.

Along the shores of Northwest Harbor, on Deer Isle, where my house is, no visible relic remains—no wharf, no loft or warehouse, no timbers of old vessels. No appreciable boat is afloat in the harbor. One spot on the northern shore is remembered as "the old steamboat landing," though no actual evidence remains. The pastures and mowings that used to reach back up to the farmplaces are now grown with trees and bushes. Some of the folk who live in the white houses are part of the old world, they have been seamen and shipwrights, and were brought up in that life of hand-work and self-sustaining economy. If you need a specialist of that sort, you can still find one. But none have any more business in the particular region they were nurtured in. They own no boats, dig no clams, catch no fish. They plant very few seeds. But they can tell of those other times. A fleet of sloops used to lie over along the southern shore—and they can remember the Morse-built *Linnie-Belle* and the *Neva* and others known for their prowess. Schooners came and went, and some lay moored all winter, frozen into the ice. The oldest memories go back to the square-riggers, the trading brigs of the eighties. Only half a century ago they used to see the beautiful three-masters at anchor off the harbor mouth, near Gull Ledge—specially the *Ella Pierce Thurlow*, the finest of all fore-and-afters. If any vessel of such size appeared there now it would be nothing less than a ghost, an apparition out of *The Ancient Mariner* or a tale by Poe.

The *Ella Pierce Thurlow* off Northwest Harbor—the finest of all
fore-and-afters

THIRTEEN

FAREWELL AND HAIL

With the quality of our desires, thoughts, and wonder proportioned to our infinite littleness we measure even time itself by our own stature. Imprisoned in the house of personal illusions thirty centuries in mankind's history seem less to look back upon than thirty years of our own life.

Joseph Conrad

OLD PEOPLE see times in the mirror of their disillusion. Prospects that were once bright and challenging are now ended. The enterprises they dreamed of and shared no longer flourish, and, instead, a conviction of decline and death takes over. The old seafarer of the Anglo-Saxon era lamented that the great days were ended and the heroes were all dead. So perspective is needed to give the steady and whole and somewhat inhuman vision that wisdom calls for. After a lifetime with the old people, old ways, old stories, the valedictory mood is inescapable.

How much is mere sentiment and nostalgia, how much ranges on the side of truth, is a problem with no final answer. But truth in the absolute is pretty grim stuff. Men have always been at their best under the spell of illusion, following out their dreams, playing for mortal stakes. And they seem to have been at their happiest in close association with what we call nature. City dwellers may have renounced nature, often by necessity rather than choice; a few philosophers proclaim their hatred for it; but most of mankind sees its happiness in terms of green fields and forests and wave-washed shores. The great good place is serene with gardens and flowers and sunny glades; Shangri-La is in the high mountains. To every transcendental visionary and poet from Blake to D. H. Lawrence all the good and worth of life, all that man could ever attain of joy and beauty, lay in that vision of natural felicity. And even now, in these positivistic and scientific times, most people yearn for the old wildness of mountains and forests or a stretch of vast seacoast with crashing waves.

Illusion, no doubt. The geological forces are what they are—as are all other doings on or in the earth. The mystic implications give us delight as though we were watching a show in a theater with willing belief, letting our hearts be beguiled, playing, crying, laughing as the clever author and showman demands.

In the Maine woods, in early summer, the hermit thrush sings. He is alone and remote, and when you hear him you are in a very quiet place among spruce trees, with no house or road near. If you hear him plainly, with the forest silence all about you, you feel the presence of such mystic beauty that your only language for it is the language of divinity. You have inevitably a religious experience. But the bird with that miraculous song, first in one key, then in another, like the notes that innocent people would attribute to God himself, is only a bird like other birds, making his habitual noise for some natural ecological purpose, which may be explained as one of the truths science is in charge of. In the light of that truth, is your glimpse of divine beauty merely a sentimental delusion? Are all your yearnings for some sort of natural felicity the same?

A more up-to-date mystique would say that though the beauty of the song which so beguiled us is a mere accidental illusion, the true divinity of this or any other bird is to be seen in his very existence on earth after uncounted centuries of evolution. Truth is indeed grand and astonishing, and becomes more so as the universe reveals itself to the mind and reach of man. But what the beauty is, and why we listen to bird songs or look for glimpses of blue sea and white breakers or windblown headlands, is a question that always just escapes analysis. It inevitably suggests something primitive and instinctual and perhaps hopelessly sentimental in us.

The fact is that we are all living in fear of the loss of that old heritage, the clean and uncontaminated country world of our fathers. The natural things are in truth dwindling. River waters are poisoned, and even the bays are empty of fish. It is hard to believe in the harvest of earlier times, the clams that used to multiply in every mud-flat, the flounders that fed a whole population, the ground fish—cod, haddock, hake, pollock—that a man could fill his dory with. The birds are vanishing, the bald eagles, and the ospreys—and even forest birds like the warblers and thrushes. That haunting song of the hermit is receding into the silence. Yet the starlings and cowbirds flourish, and crows and cormorants and the ubiquitous herring gulls who can thrive on garbage. In a man-dominated ecology new evolutionary forces are at work. More and more nature has to be invented and cultivated and preserved by tricks of stagecraft: in a not too remote future we may inhabit a vast Disneyland, and take our pleasure in observing pneumatic wildlife and plastic mountains. The process is in fact very apparent—in the mountains already tailored for skiers, with lifts and heated shelters and artificial snow, in the streams stocked and arranged for fishing, in the so-called camp grounds with plumbing, or in the salt-water marinas where boats are handled and parked like automobiles.

People in greater and greater numbers, power and equipment more ingenious, and the old bucolic illusion seems almost too remote for memory. *Walden* is merely a dream. So is the old coast of Maine. Many will cling to it in sentiment and longing in order to escape the anxieties and compulsions of a too crowded world. For years to come our frontier regions will be the refuges not for wildlife or game but for people looking for the lost Eden. More of the coast may in time become a national preserve, as part of Mount Desert now is, with guards and picnic sites and nature walks. Weekenders will whisk to and fro to the islands by air. Local business will devote itself to supplying and maintaining the seasonal visitors. If our future technology can restrain its ingenuities some sort of recreational balance may be achieved.

But whoever lived in this region as a boy a half century ago, before the First World War, is possessed by the memory to an almost mystic degree. He has long ago drunk the milk of Paradise. If he came as I did every summer from earliest childhood he lived the year round in a vision of a

211 of FAREWELL AND HAIL

region so pure and serene that it seemed like a special creation of its own. The steamer voyage was a translation from the mortal realms of heat and dust to a separate world on the frontier of heaven. The icy morning air, the breakers creaming along granite shores, the silent dark forest, the islands folding away into the mysterious distances, gray sails in the offing—it was a time of happiness mounting into ecstasy. And then the harbor of home, the white houses, the melody of voices, the mowings, the flowering pastures, the cows, sheep, open barns, the kindness of welcome, the courtesy, the friends. I recollect George Dodge's weathered face and pale eyes as he spontaneously welcomed my mother and sisters in their city clothes: "Why damn it all to hell, I'm glad to see you folks again."

A world designed specially for boys. Any map for pirates or treasure seekers or adventurers need only recreate almost any square mile of that coast, with secret deep-water coves, hidden beaches of golden sand, headlands, ledges smothered in misty breakers, dark mossy forests, granite hilltops like miniature mountains, and always the mystery of remote shores, with the wrecks of great vessels and driftwood and flotsam stacked in century-old heaps above the surge of tide. The revelations are endless—every point hides the unknown, every bight and cranny in the cliffs opens a hidden treasure. You are led on and on always with hope, not for tangible objects so much as for some glimpse of secret wonders that no man has ever yet had. Again and again you have a sense of absolute discovery, as though you were the first in all creation to pass that lovely promontory and set eyes on the promised land beyond.

And for a boy of course it was a world of human prowess. The men he saw were able men. They handled their sea stuff with perfect knowledge as though they were somehow born that way. The boy watched and practised. He learned to skull with a single oar—he spent hours flubbing round in secret before catching and perfecting the trick of it so that he could propel a dory across a harbor with silent and apparently careless ease. He learned to row standing and facing forward the way all fisherman did, a back-tiring and unnatural action that demanded years of conditioning. He learned about the rigging of vessels, and the use of tackles and blocks. He watched the knots and splices, and carried bits of rope to practice on. Schooners and sloops lay at the wharves and were in a constant state of repair, and if the boy were in luck he might get himself hoisted in a bosun's chair to a masthead to reeve a new peak halyard. He learned the arts of caulking, watched the play of mallet and iron, the long strands of twisted oakum being pounded home with the rhythmic thunk-thunk that was part of the familiar music of shipwork. He saw the everlasting scraping of weeds and rust and old paint; the sandings and repaintings never ended. Some of the hulks seemed as ancient as the Ark, and were as indigenous to the landscape as the wharves and houses.

And the talk, the voices, going on and on like a quiet stream, reminiscent, pungent, profane, ironic, funny, a melody to go with the thunk of the mallet underneath and the whoosh of sandpaper along the sheer strake. Paintbrushes made no noise and encouraged the most talk. "Well, you recollect old Pearl Trundy, he had about as much brain as a peahen or maybe less, but he was one o' them hearty fellers, he'd start talkin' to you a half a mile away—first thing you know you'd hear him holler 'How's your pa? How's your ma?' He was always askin' about your pa and ma—didn't make no difference who you were. Well, he had one o' them stone sloops—you don't see 'em much any more, but I tell you they was the meanest, crankiest contraptions that ever floated—God knows why they ever built 'em except being one-masted they had more hold space, but Jesus! you couldn't sail 'em light at all with that mains'l big as a circus tent, and loaded with stone they scared hell out o' you. It took just such a man as Pearl to handle 'em—all muscle and no brain. Oh, he had her for years—I recollect seeing her in and out of Tenant's Harbor there, and it was always a wonder to me he kept her afloat as long as he did. All he had mostly for crew was a man and a boy or two—I guess he used his own boys all he could. Anyway, they hired him to take the stone out for that wharf on Little Babcock Island, it was when that boardinghouse and cottages were there—feller named Ettrick from Boston had the notion of making a resort out of it, and he got the old *General Knox* to call, but there wasn't no wharf for her. They had to take folks off in a kind of a scow they'd built a-purpose for it. Well, they got Pearl to bring the stone—leastways he started with it. Next thing anyone knew about him he come into Owl's Head Cove there in a dory, him and his boys—said she'd gone down right under them, said she dove like a damned submarine; that's how he said it—dove like a damned submarine. It was the first day of June and I remember it well—one of those smokey green sou'westers,

and I come out of Rockland in that little packet used to belong to Ned Avery; all we had set was just the fores'l and
stays'l—she was the *Martha Mullins*, you may recollect
her, an able enough vessel, but that stone sloop of Pearl's,
why she warn't as able as one o' those old driftwood scows
used to carry the firewood in to Rockport there for the
limestone burning. Pearl, though, he never had , much
sense."

A world and time spun out in endless reminiscence.
From the stone sloops to the driftwooders—and on through
all manner of seagoing eccentrics and oddities, always
hovering about the infinite ways of ships and weather.

My early days were spent on a small island called Mill
Island, with a shingled cottage on top of a great high rock
above the water, and being an island it was a complete little
world, whole, separate, uncontaminated. In its half-mile
length was every natural felicity native to the coast. The
high gray cliff where the house was, with a glimpse southward to the sea's horizon, the new-moon curve of beach
below, sheltered enough for boats to land, then rocky
points, shores of polished stones, pockets of pure sand,
mossy glades, dark mysteries of forest, and on the far side,
alone and forever abandoned, a wrecked schooner, lying
canted on the sand, washed by the high tide, with masts and
rigging still aloft. A boy could swing dizzily out into space
on a halyard and back again to the slanting deck.

A trip round the shores seemed always like a voyage of
discovery. New driftwood washed in on the beaches, wild
creatures carried on their affairs—ducks and loons and
seals; fishhawks soared and circled above the tidal pond
on the inner side and dove for flounders like guided

On the far side, alone and forever abandoned, a wrecked schooner
lying canted on the sand, washed by the high tide

rockets. At certain tides the water rushed out—or in—
with the small fury of a reversing falls. Minnows flocked
into the salt-marsh streams, clams throve in the flats,
flounders lived in the channels, as well as sculpins and a
few skates and eels. At low water a wagon and team could
reach the island by a hard pull along beaches and rocky
lanes and over muddy bars, but at high water the whole
place seemed to preserve itself in perfect purity. Everything about it was washed clean. The stones, sands, shells,
mosses, trees, grass, were all perfect in their own colors
and substance, all newly minted and somehow polished by
the sea-wind and water. And the water itself was a cold
glinting green, too cold for anyone but boys to swim in.

> *Oh were there an island*
> *Though never so wild. . . .*

Perhaps a boy's world will always be there. The little
island still is, untouched these many years. But all such
things depend on who see them, and what they see. Almost everyone responds instinctively to the natural fe-
licities, but in this latter part of the twentieth century they
have relatively little philosophical hold over people. Land-
scapes are primarily recreational diversions, seen from a
moving car or the terrace of an inn or restaurant; they are
to be enjoyed as views, and represent a pleasant change
from the serious professions and careers carried on in cities
and suburbs. Some kinds of landscape, like mountains and
sea, are a challenge to athletes and sportsmen and adventurers, but the old natural pantheism of the romantic poets
and philosophers has gone the way of all religion. It is still
a beguiling sentiment, it invokes hopes and dreams in simple

hearts, but the weight of modern scientific thought, whether positivistic, behavioristic, or existential, is solidly against it. Man's chief business from now on is to master his surroundings and redesign and rebuild them for his own uses. And of course in the process he will inevitably redesign himself.

If this old world seems to exist chiefly as a subject for nostalgia, the truth remains that it did once dominate the minds and bodies of many generations of men. Its prophet for most of our people was William Wordsworth the poet, who could express his passionate awareness of divine beauty in all natural things—the setting sun over still waters, the sound of a waterfall in spring, the arc of a rainbow. But perhaps his New England followers came closer to us. Bryant and Whittier, Thoreau and Emerson. All through the last century the belief was strong that men and nature could live in harmony, that some wise divinity had designed and arranged the visible world with a benevolent and beautiful logic that was at least being perceived. Even the findings of Darwin and other scientists could be read as confirmation of this faith: the word evolution itself had a hopeful ring to it.

And from the point of view of simple-hearted New Englanders, at least, the natural world functioned as though it reflected and answered to a divine order. The roll of the seasons, the wondrous yearly renewal of earth, the closeness of men to their surroundings, the planting and reaping and harvesting, the strength and honesty of handwork, the collaboration of animals, the native materials, the self-determination and self-respect—all these and many other ways and habits actually existed. The people on the old coast of Maine were not romantic philosophers or poets—they were not at all bookish or self-conscious—but they did seem to provide the evidence on which philosophy could build. They illustrated what could be done when the right people and the right place and climate and conditions all collaborated in a harmonious and at best beautiful way of life.

As for the future, we know only that it will be inconceivable. In a few years more people will be living on earth than have lived altogether in all the ages of human history —so we are told by prophetic statisticians. In time man himself will function more and more electronically, and what we think of in our innocence as human nature will be subject to planned design and control. The little world I have remembered in these pages will soon seem as remote as the world of the cliff dwellers of Mesa Verde now seems to us. What is to come is our destiny—and for all I know it may be a blessed one. What has gone deserves an affectionate farewell.

THE AUTHOR

ALTHOUGH he was born on Long Island (Sept. 23, 1901) and brought up in Dobbs Ferry and New York City, Gerald Warner Brace has lived most of his life in New England.

Following his graduation from Amherst, he studied architecture at Harvard for a year, then took his M.A. and Ph.D. in English. He has taught at Radcliffe, Williams, Dartmouth, Mount Holyoke, and Amherst, and is now Professor of English at Boston University.

He is, he says, much given to mountain climbing, skiing, and sailing boats. He lives in Belmont, Mass., and spends his summers at Deer Isle, Maine, where he does most of his writing but spends as much time as he can sailing the 31-foot sloop he designed.

He has written ten novels.